Beyond Experience

Revised Edition

Beyond Experience

The Experiential Approach to Cross-Cultural Education

Revised Edition

Edited by THEODORE GOCHENOUR
First edition edited by Donald Batchelder and Elizabeth G. Warner

INTERCULTURAL PRESS, INC.

For information, contact:
Intercultural Press, Inc.
P.O. Box 700
Yarmouth, Maine 04096 USA

Book design and production by Patty J. Topel
Cover design by Ralph Copeland

Printed in the United States of America

98 97 96 95 94 93   1 2 3 4 5 6

Library of Congress Cataloging-in-Publication Data

Beyond experience/[edited by] Theodore Gochenour.
   p.   cm.
   Revision of 1977 ed.
   Includes bibliographical references
   ISBN 1-877864-24-2
   1. Multicultural education. I. Gochenour, Theodore.

LC1099.B49   1993
370.19'6—dc20   93-34374
                                                     CIP

Table of Contents

PART ONE IDEAS

Note to Our Readers

In 1992 The Experiment in International Living changed its name to World Learning, Inc., in order to reflect more accurately the reality of the present organization. While we respect the rationale for the change, we were also presented with a dilemma. Not only is the original name venerable, i.e., familiar to vast numbers of people both inside and outside the education profession, but it is integral to this book.

The first edition was published while the organization was still called by its original name and, more importantly, was specifically intended to embody an approach to experiential education special to The Experiment as it was constituted at the time (1977). The book is therefore laced with references to "The Experiment in International Living," "The Experiment," and "Experimenters" (not to mention the acronym "EIL").

We had to consider carefully whether or not to change those references. In the end, given the familiarity of the Experiment name and, especially, given that the book was first published when the references were appropriate, we have decided to maintain them, with an occasional reminder of the change.

While the book has been extensively revised, some original materials deleted and new ones added, we feel it captures the spirit of The Experiment as it existed at the time of the book's original publication. We are, of course, aware that the orientation toward experiential education embodied in it still characterizes much of the educational program at World Learning, but we have decided that maintaining the references to The Experiment is appropriate because it both fits the history of the publication and reflects the ethos in which the ideas were generated.

Preface

Those of us in the 1970s who worked at The Experiment in International Living, now named World Learning, Inc., were delighted when it became possible to publish *Beyond Experience*. For years, people interested in experiential learning and cross-cultural training had asked us for examples of the sort of things we did. Finally, instead of photocopies of articles and exercises, we had a real book to offer. I doubt that any of us could have predicted that our efforts might still be of interest to people so many years later.

The supply of the first edition of *Beyond Experience* never kept up with the demand. As the years went by, the question arose as to whether a new edition might be needed instead of a reprint of the original. Meanwhile, many other things were happening at The Experiement; a year here and a year there slipped by amidst other priorities. In 1991, the organization decided to discontinue The Experiment Press. One very positive outcome of that decision was an agreement with Intercultural Press to publish *Beyond Experience* in a revised edition.

Readers familiar with the original will find that much remains the same in this new version. The articles continue to be grouped in three broad divisions: Ideas, Activities (formerly called Exercises), and Assessment. Some pieces have been moved about for a more logical placement, and small changes in the text have been made here and there. A couple of articles which did not seem to quite fit with the overall body of material have been dropped. I am particularly pleased that this edition contains some new material reflecting more recent practice at World Learning. Grateful thanks are due to each contributor, past and present, whose thoughts and efforts are reflected in these pages.

There is something which might be called the "Experiment spirit" underlying the articles in *Beyond Experience*. After twenty-five years of association with the organization, I have given up trying to define it more exactly. Somehow it seems to come through, at times articulated, at other times more implied than stated. One of the earliest efforts to capture in writing something of this spirit appears in the article by Donald Batchelder, "The Green Banana." It seems to me a fine way to launch the reader into what we hope will be useful, provocative, and enjoyable reading in the pages to come.

Theodore Gochenour
West Dummerston, VT

The Green Banana
Donald Batchelder

Any comprehensive list of the fruits of learning should be expanded to include the green banana. No major revision of the curriculum is necessary, but amid the talk of learning and discovery, possibilities should be available to allow discovery to take place.

Although it might have happened anywhere, my encounter with the green banana started on a steep mountain road in the interior of Brazil. My ancient Jeep was straining up through spectacular countryside when the radiator began to leak, ten miles from the nearest mechanic. The overheated engine forced me to stop at the next hamlet, which consisted of a small store and a scattering of houses. People gathered around to look. Three fine streams of hot water spouted from holes in the jacket of the radiator. "That's easy to fix," a man said. He sent a boy running for some green bananas. He patted me on the shoulder, assuring me that everything would work out. "Green bananas," he smiled. Everyone agreed.

We exchanged pleasantries while I mulled over the ramifications of the green banana. Asking questions would betray my ignorance, so I remarked on the beauty of the terrain. Huge rock formations, like Sugar Loaf in Rio, rose up all around us. "Do you see that tall one right over there?" asked my benefactor, pointing to a particularly tall, slender pinnacle of dark rock. "That rock marks the center of the world."

I looked to see if he were teasing me, but his face was serious. He in turn inspected me carefully to be sure I grasped the significance of his statement. The occasion demanded some show of recognition on my part. "The center of the world?" I repeated, trying to convey interest if not complete acceptance. He nodded. "The absolute center. Everyone around here knows it."

At that moment the boy returned with my green bananas. The man sliced one in half and pressed the cut end against the radiator jacket. The banana melted into a glue against the hot metal, plugging the leaks instantly. Everyone laughed at my astonishment. They refilled my radiator and gave me extra bananas to take along. An hour later, after one more application of green banana, my radiator and I reached our destination. The local mechanic smiled. "Who taught you about the green banana?" I named the hamlet. "Did they show you the rock marking the center of the world?" he asked. I assured him they had. "My grandfather came from there," he said. "The exact center. Everyone around here has always known about it."

I took time to internalize the possible meanings of these events. A roadway led to temporary difficulty, resulting in a discovery which resolved the problem while opening up a whole new perspective of shared belief and speculation. As a product of American higher education, I had never paid the slightest attention to the green banana, except to regard it as a fruit whose time had not yet come. Suddenly on that mountain road, its time and my need had converged. But as I reflected on it further, I realized that the green banana had been there all along. Its time reached back to the very origins of the banana. The people in that hamlet had known about it for years. My own time had come in relation to it. This chance encounter showed me the special genius of those people and the special potential of the green banana. I had been wondering for some time about those episodes of clarity which educators like to call "learning moments," and I knew I had just experienced two of them at once.

The import of the rock marking the center of the world took a while to filter through. I had initially doubted their claim, knowing for a fact that the center was located somewhere in New England. After all, my grandfather had come from there. But gradually I realized they had a valid belief, a universal concept, and I agreed with them. We tend to define the center as that special place where we are known, where we know others, where things mean much to us, and where we ourselves have both identity and meaning: family, school, town, and local region. The lesson which gradually filtered through was the simple concept that every place has special meanings for the people in it; every place represents the center of the world. The number of such centers is incalculable, and no one student or traveler can experience all of them; but once a conscious breakthrough to a second center is made, a perspective is established and a lifelong journey collecting centers of the world can begin.

If some of the goals of education in modern times are to open up possibilities for discovery and expand learning and the chance for mutual acceptance and recognition in a wider world, it may be important to offer students a perspective on their own immediate center of the world by enabling them to participate sensitively as cross-cultural sojourners to the center of someone else's world. The cultures of the world are full of unexpected green bananas with special value and meaning. They have been there for ages, ripening slowly, perhaps waiting patiently for our students to come along to encounter them. There are people there who will interpret the special meanings, give them perspective, combine ideas in new ways, and slice old concepts to answer modern questions. Personal discoveries converge in a flow of learning moments, developing a healthy tug-of-war between that original center of the world from whence the student comes and the new center being experienced. Eventually the student has a strong sense of identity in two centers, in two cultures. Both have special meanings, and both the self-awareness and cultural awareness of the student have been significantly increased.

There are many ways to go about this. No single formula is suitable for all students. One program which has been taking students to the center of the world for sixty years is provided by The Experiment in International Living. The approach is directly concerned with the roadways which lead to the interior of the host culture, the conscious recognition of the importance of being in the center of their world, and the attitudes and behaviors which demonstrate that it is a good place and we are lucky to be there.

Throughout the entire exposure in the center of that new world, the way is left open for each Experimenter to discover himself or herself and to be discovered in turn. In our quest for personal and cultural awareness, for appreciation of the patterns and meanings of other cultures, and for the values of international understanding, every student should have an opportunity to try out those steep roadways to the interior. A green banana is waiting for each of them, there at the center of the world. Every person's grandfather came from there, and everyone around there has always known about it.

Printed in *New York Parents' League Review*, under the title, "Ripening at the Center of the World," 3, no. 1 (Spring 1974): 26-29.
Reprinted, March 1974, in *Odyssey*, Newsletter of The Experiment in International Living 3, no. 2 (March 1974).

Beyond Experience: The Experiential Approach to Cross-Cultural Education
Anne Janeway

In the late seventies, when this book was first published, it seemed necessary to state the obvious: that there is an underlying purpose for the current interest in cross-cultural communication and education. Humanity, we hoped, was moving toward a spirit of global togetherness in a world which already recognized and affirmed the interrelatedness of all the people who share the planet. And for many of us who had chosen to work in the area of cross-cultural education, there was a deep commitment to acknowledging, respecting, and appreciating the cultural diversity that characterizes and profoundly enriches the world.

At that time, we saw cross-cultural education as a new field of endeavor which addressed in practical and theoretical ways the challenges of living and working in a multicultural world. As a member of the staff of The Experiment in International Living, working on a daily basis with participants and students who were involved in a wide range of intercultural endeavors (from program administrators in refugee camps in Thailand and Indonesia to high school students living for a summer with a family in Mexico), we were challenged to design and implement educational programs to help individuals prepare for effective service in a variety of cultural settings. Our educational approach seemed significant to us in its practicality and, like all approaches one might choose, reflected assumptions we had made in our attempt to answer a number of difficult questions, one of the most important of which was: what leads human beings from a state of fear, ignorance, and distrust (if not hatred) of those who are culturally different to a state in which they want to understand, communicate, and connect? And once this desire of heart and mind is present, what converts it to action? As one way of responding or seeking answers to these questions, The Experiment chose the way of experiential education. We saw our program designs as practical, as real ways to lead a student to say, "Something has happened to me. I see differently. I understand more deeply. I act in new ways. I am not the same. I am less limited and more able to include another's reality in my own."

Today, cultural diversity is a recognized fact. It is not necessary to call each other's attention to the fact that we live in a world of many cultures, nor that, if we do not take the responsibility for learning to live in increasing harmony with diverse peoples, everyone—including ourselves —will suffer. However, the need for healing in intercultural conflicts (including issues of race, homophobia, and gender) and the need for caring relationships among human beings who work together in this shrinking world is as great as it has ever been. Cross-cultural work calls us more emphatically than ever.

What this demands of us as teachers is an approach which recognizes and addresses not only the intellect but, to the extent we are able, the whole person. It is work that calls upon heart and mind, body and soul. In this we acknowledge the nature of cross-cultural experience with its inevitable challenges to one's personal identity as well as the willingness needed to confront the pain of limitation and ignorance intrinsic in the process of growth. Many deep feelings are involved in intercultural work, and its spiritual dimension is finally being recognized as well.

All this is important because we cannot find the harmony we seek (or even the peaceful coexistence that we need) without connecting in some way to the deeper aspects of ourselves. The value of this process in the end, however, lies in reclaiming the essential humanity in ourselves and in others. The expression of our common humanity lies in empathy and a truer understanding—understanding that comes from the heart.

The exercises and articles that follow represent opportunities to extend and deepen our learning. All share a common commitment to an expansion of awareness, of consciousness of oneself in relation to a larger whole, and to taking responsibility for acting in harmony with what one comes to know. All involve an experiential approach to cross-cultural education.

Part One

IDEAS

1

Seven Concepts in Cross-Cultural Interaction: A Training Design

Theodore Gochenour and Anne Janeway

The following pages describe an approach to cross-cultural training which has been tested with graduate students at the School for International Training of The Experiment in International Living. Our discussion concerns the primary assumptions underlying this approach and a conceptual outline of its parts.

The design of this training is based on the belief that the individual involved in cross-cultural interaction is central to the success of that interaction. While this may appear self-evident, many training programs, in fact, seem to lose sight of that reality. In this program, the focus is on the *process* of an individual's interaction with people in an unfamiliar culture and, especially, upon his or her awareness of that process. Our emphasis on interactive process does not exclude the presence of specific information about a given culture. Exercises and readings about a culture or about any aspect of a culture may be created or assigned as the need is felt. We have generally used the training approach presented here with participants who have already had personal experience in one or more cultures. The concepts have helped to clarify and consolidate their past experiences and have provided a framework for understanding cultural interactions in the future. While the primary focus of this training is cross-cultural interaction, it should be noted that many participants have felt that these seven concepts also usefully describe a process of personal maturation and growth.

As stated above, our cross-cultural training approach stresses the interactive process and is based on the assumption that stages or conditions which occur in all intercultural situations can be identified, without reference to specifics of time and place. We feel that these stages or conditions hold true without regard to the actual *content* of the process. A new culture can be met at a level of bare survival or at a level of advanced preparation. In either case, and at levels between, quite definable and similar stages of involvement are experienced. These stages occur whatever the culture, whatever the level of preparation, and however we, as arriving outsiders, affect existing situations.

These seven stages have been identified and defined to be broadly inclusive. Each stage should be seen as containing within it any number of implied levels, ranging from the simple and primitive to the advanced and subtle. The seven stages inevitably suggest an evolution over time as well as a procession through the process. While it is quite possible for some elements to occur almost simultaneously, or in no set order, we feel that a successful cross-cultural interaction would demonstrate that all the stages are encountered and can be identified.

This training concept contains a number of expressed or implied assumptions, as do all human endeavors. Perhaps our most important assumption concerns the purpose of cross-cultural preparation: the development of an appreciative, nonexploitative relationship with people of another culture. The objective of this approach is not improved commerce, national advantage, or religious conversion (to name but a few reasons for going abroad or wanting to be more effective cross-culturally), but solely as an end in itself, as a means toward building a closer human community. Thus, the term "success," used above, should be read to mean the degree to which a person is able to enter into respectful, appreciative (though not necessarily admiring) relationships within a culture other than his or her own, and discover some values that have personal significance and a sense of common humanity.

The seven elements which form our conceptual framework fall into two groups of three, with one bridging element between them. The first three are:

1. Establish contact and essential communication
2. Establish bona fides and be accepted (i.e., allowed to exist)
3. Observe what is going on and sort out meanings

These initial conditions constitute sheer survival elements. If we think of cross-cultural interaction at the dramatic level of arriving on an unknown island populated by hostile headhunters, these three stages would be apparent to the person involved. In a more likely situation, where a person arrives to take up a job assignment overseas, these steps will still occur. The *content* of the two experiences, however, will be vastly different.

To explore these further, stages one and two occur almost automatically, assuming one avoids the stew pot of the headhunters or, in the more familiar situation, early rejection by the locals or culture shock of such dimensions as to prevent any further development of relationships. We normally arrive and some kind of contact is established. However, since we inevitably lack the depth of perception and understanding we will eventually develop, we often feel things are just happening to us. *Essential communication* refers to meeting our most basic and immediate needs *in that situation*. Our awareness is almost completely focused on personal needs which range from obtaining the essentials of life to getting directions to a tourist attraction and tend to arise at the point of first contact.

There is one critical difference, however, between the first two stages. At stage two, the fact that we are accepted *on someone else's terms* begins to complicate the picture. Our own view of the world, or our idea of ourselves and of why we are there, does not determine how we are accepted. We are accepted—or not—into someone else's scheme of things and defined by their frame of reference. The way we respond determines in large measure our future relationships in that culture. Even at the earliest steps in cross-cultural interaction, our thoughts and emotions as well as our actions shape the future.

At stage three, observing what is going on and sorting out meanings, we begin to affect our environment more consciously.

This process is time-consuming and requires both skill in observation and a knowledge of oneself. From the standpoint of awareness, it marks the time when we begin consciously and unconsciously looking outside of ourselves and beyond our immediate concerns. The process of trying to discover meaning in someone else's reality is very much colored by our understanding of ourselves. Our personal interests and habits determine what we observe, and our prior knowledge and associations affect our interpretation of it.

Stages one and two happen *to* the individual and elicit an uninformed response. At stage three the ability of the person to reflect and respond more deliberately becomes important. Concept four bridges the first three and the last three stages, which will not come about at all except through conscious volition on the part of the individual.

Stage four is:

4. Establish a role within the role definitions of the host society

Just as we are accepted or not on someone else's cultural terms, we can establish a role for ourselves only within the conceptual categories assigned to us by the host culture, not by our own. We may think we have come there to be a "friend," or "student," or "lover of humanity," yet in the eyes of our hosts we may be an "imperialist," or "infidel," or "just another tourist." In effect, we are assigned a role to play within that culture. Often it is a role close enough to the one we defined for ourselves to be comfortable. Over time we may learn how to change our role or how to carry out several different roles. We may even have some influence on how the host culture defines roles, but we cannot impose our role on another society. As that culture defines us, so does it act toward us and expect us to act.

Grouping stage four with the first three, we have a picture of a good many people who can spend time abroad without being touched deeply and without changing any established value or belief. Such persons might be very knowledgeable about their host culture, speak the language well, and be engaged in productive activities. They might also be tourists on a bus. The *content* of the two conditions is considerably different.

Becoming established in a place and knowledgeable about it, and acquiring a role there, inevitably confront the individual with situa-

tions and interactions which offer opportunities for deeper perceptions and more informed understandings. They are latent in the
situation. Some cross-cultural sojourners, however, reach a comfortable but relatively limited level of interaction and stay there. An
adequate language skill remains flawed, but adequate. An opinion,
once formed, feels too "right" to challenge or change. The locals
continue to seem alien and outlandish in their beliefs, even if we learn
a few rules to deal with them.

For many, this describes all the cross-cultural interaction which
is desirable or required. The question is whether the process need
stop here or whether there may be somewhere further to go. We
answer this question by referring to our underlying assumption
about what constitutes success. We do not mean to imply that it is
wrong to approach cross-cultural interaction (and training) for purposes of reaching another goal, such as economic development or the
conduct of diplomacy. While utilitarian goals have their place, we
believe it is equally valid to pursue a nonutilitarian purpose. The
choice belongs to the individual and institution concerned. If that
choice is toward finding values within the host culture which might
challenge or change those which one already holds—toward becoming persons no longer culturally bound in one frame of reference—
then we feel that three additional stages remain. As in earlier stages,
these elements may occur simultaneously or in a different order, but
on close examination, they will be found to be present. Similarly, the
richness, profundity, and specialness of the experience will vary
from person to person and context to context.

The final stages are:

5. Conscious knowledge of oneself—as a center, as a cultural
   being, and as one taking responsibility
6. Conscious development of needed attributes and skills—
   mental, emotional, and physical
7. Conscious establishment of self-sustaining and meaningful
   relationships within the host culture

Because it requires volition and effort to go beyond a plateau of
functional existence in another culture, it can immediately be seen
that success depends upon the internal state of the individual. We
believe that the personal growth which results from cross-cultural

interaction is an aspect of a larger process of expansion taking place in the person's consciousness. In applying this training design in student programs, we have used the word *center*. We are aware of ourselves as a center when our self-definition lies within us but is apart from our ever-changing mental, emotional, and physical states. For some, no such center exists. They may be able to accept that their identity is not dependent upon the condition of their bodies, but find it harder to accept that it is not made up somehow in the totality of what they feel and think. For others, the concept is immediately meaningful and powerful, often accompanied by both a sense of release and by an increased ability to focus personal energies.

In stage five, a "conscious knowledge of oneself—as a center, as a cultural being, and as one taking responsibility," is the most difficult concept to understand and accept. In the sense meant here, this self-consciousness does not refer to nervousness, ego strength, or self-absorption. The self-aware person we are attempting to describe is one sensitive to and observant of both external and internal processes, one who has achieved some autonomy and effectiveness from a perspective which places the passage of events— and one's reactions to them—in some broader context. This person is one who seeks to share. To be conscious of oneself at this level is not easy, nor does it just happen even if one has an idea of the process. If, for example, we define ourselves in terms of the roles we have learned or been conditioned to play in our own society, it is difficult if not impossible to risk new and perhaps contradictory roles. If our self-definition, however, lies apart from our acquired roles, beliefs, and passing feelings, we are able to enter into new relationships and new experiences with greater confidence and fewer impediments. As has been said by others, we are truly dominated by everything with which we identify.

The second aspect of this concept—knowing oneself as a cultural being—is easier to understand, at least in intellectual terms. We are a product of the culture in which we have participated for most if not all of our lives. The problem here lies in accepting that we *are* acculturated, whether we like it or not, and then in learning how to handle the fact that our habits and emotions are harder to change than our ideas.

The third element we have mentioned is responsibility. We feel that it is a clear indication of maturation—with an attendant positive impact on the ability to communicate cross-culturally—when a person grasps the reality of personal responsibility. This means that, while we are not necessarily responsible for a particular circumstance or event, we *are* responsible for its effect on us. In turn, we are responsible for our effect, seen or not seen, conscious or unconscious, desired or not desired, on others. If our presence is disruptive, we are responsible for that disruption, and no amount of goodwill or positive intention changes that fact. It is when we take appropriate responsibility for every event in which we are engaged, every response we make, every inward reaction we record, that we can truly be said to have begun to move out of the confinements of our acquired habits, attitudes, and values.

Motivated toward effective cross-cultural interaction, a person who is reasonably self-aware and functioning well in the culture can move consciously to a level where his or her values can in part be derived from the host society. This calls for an awareness of what is needed and a commitment to new learning and conscious growth or, as we say, conscious development of needed attributes and skills. The principal difference between the development of skills at stage five and observing what is going on and sorting out meanings in stage three (which, of course, can be quite sophisticated) is the conscious movement toward the ultimate goal in stage seven. We want to be further involved, to delve deeper, to find something in the other culture that touches us in a satisfying and meaningful way. We know ourselves better, and we see what facilitates or hinders greater knowing and involvement, and we work consciously to develop the needed skills.

We may find that our bodies need further training (to sit cross-legged for hours, for example, or to learn to enjoy eating with one's hands). We may need to develop greater intellectual skills to reach an in-depth understanding of our hosts. The most obvious might be to move from a serviceable facility in the language to a level where we comprehend its nuances. To reach stage seven, however, it is necessary to go far beyond developing these relatively obvious skills—we must begin to comprehend another's perceptions of reality, both physical and spiritual. This development constitutes a continual challenge, for the complexities of another's world are often indescribably subtle when approached from the outside, and years of contact are needed to understand them. Skill development is also required in the affective realm. Because new situations are generally threatening, it is necessary to build emotional muscle with which to cope with stress. A lack of the kind of privacy one is accustomed to, for example, is not only a physical reality, it is an emotional one as well. Unless we recognize the internal effect and consciously search for ways to deal with it, our emotions may block us from seeing what is truly happening and from recognizing what is involved in terms of the host culture.

We would like to point out that the development of self-sustaining relationships in and deep engagement with another culture is not the same as "going native," a condition of personal and cultural disorientation. We believe that something of real value is gained when we know ourselves to be products of one culture, yet affected and enlarged by our involvement in another. If "no man is an island," then our knowledge of other lands increases our knowledge of ourselves.

Training programs based on this conceptual framework generally use a series of exercises, readings, discussions, activities, etc. The seven concepts are abstract, so the training is designed to allow each participant the opportunity to discover his or her own personal meanings. It recognizes that the possibilities for learning at any stage are unlimited. While the content of establishing a role in Bolivia may be enormously different from establishing a role in Nigeria, both involve a similar, definable process, one which has familiar elements that can be shared with those who are anticipating a cross-cultural experience. They can then go forth with a rational developmental process in mind which enables them to assess and understand the day-to-day events as they occur and the cumulative effect of many interactions.

We believe that this conceptual framework allows participants to learn in the style that best suits them. Some prefer a more cognitive approach using readings, presentations, and discussions. Our own preference is for an experiential approach, using many of the exercises which appear in this book. Because of their diffuse and subtle nature, cross-cultural interactions go well beyond an intellectual understanding of either the process or the specifics of the situation.

The whole person is caught up and involved; the identity of the person may be fundamentally challenged; all aspects of the person—mental, emotional, physical—are affected. Effective cross-cultural training, in our view, takes this total reality into account in its design. The five values of experiential learning, described in John Wallace's article which follows, state the case clearly. It is through experiential learning—which has an impact on the whole person—that meaningful preparation can best be achieved.

2

Educational Values of Experiential Education

John A. Wallace

As an undergraduate, I submitted a geography paper which analyzed the impact of drought on the economies of certain subtropical nations and territories. It was a document filled with information about meteorological patterns, centimeters of rainfall, storage capacities of reservoirs, depths of water tables, and mortality patterns caused by starvation. The paper was judged worthy of a grade of *A* and, by academic standards, was a successful effort.

Twenty years later, I chanced to walk down the streets of Calcutta at a time when parts of India were undergoing one of their periodic famines. In the course of a fifteen-minute stroll, after a sumptuous breakfast in my hotel, I observed more than a dozen bodies being picked up from the sidewalks, strapped onto boards, and loaded into vehicles for movement to the burning *ghats*.

These two personal incidents crystallize the essence of the topic at hand—the educational values of experiential education. The knowledge I gained as a university undergraduate came from the classroom and the library. I acquired certain information, organized it into a reasonably logical flow of ideas, and emerged with the conclusion that droughts killed a lot of people. I passed the course, but was not changed in any significant way. My knowledge of droughts and famines increased intellectual awareness but produced no action, no involvement, no commitment.

My sidewalk stroll in Calcutta changed intellectual knowledge into emotional awareness. The bodies being carted away had been, a few days previously, living, thinking, sensate, dreaming human beings. Now they were dead from simple starvation, victims of drought and famine over which they had no control. The facts of my undergraduate paper had now turned into funeral pyres. And I changed. In a variety of ways during subsequent years I have given expression to this change: in work with Peace Corps groups; in helping to prepare young people participating in The Experiment's programs; in active involvement to aid the victims of one of Bangladesh's crises; in contributing to CARE and Church World Service; in the creation of The Experiment's World Issues Program, which provides two years of undergraduate study and personal involvement in critical fields such as economic and social development, ecology, peace studies, and population studies; and in helping to encourage certain graduates of our Program in Intercultural Management to apply for positions with CARE in India. These personal episodes provide specific background against which we might examine the basic principles which they exemplify.

I stress the fact that my emotional experience was preceded by intellectual study. Information I gathered for my undergraduate term paper made it possible for me to interpret what I was seeing and experiencing. Instead of ruminating ("I wonder what all those bodies were; do you suppose they were drunks who had passed out?"), I had a frame of reference which told me, "This, Wallace, is what you wrote about many years ago. Now you see what it means."

I stress this as my first point because I feel that too often we who sing the praises of experiential education are unfairly accused of offering our students a titillating variety of experiences without first insisting upon the rigorous scholarship and intellectual discipline which should precede a cross-cultural experience. Our students' cries for relevance must not tempt us to jettison our basic system of liberal (and liberating) education.

This leads us directly, however, to the second essential value of experiential education: its force as a motivator. "But why must I take two years of French?" students may querulously ask. There are several possible responses: "It's one of our requirements for a degree"; "It's good for you"; "It says in the catalogue that sociology majors need two years of a foreign language"; or, "You'll need French when you get to France in your junior year." Need I underline which student is most apt to work assiduously at meeting his or her French requirement?

It is obvious from what I have said about my Indian experience that I consider the affective influence of experiential learning to be its second major—perhaps its most important—value. In most of The Experiment programs we seek to influence students in the direction of becoming committed agents of change. It is far from coincidental, therefore, that in all our programs we build in an experiential component which covers about half the duration of the program. This is true both at the undergraduate and graduate levels. We are committed at the School for International Training to intensive predeparture intellectual study followed by an immersion experience in another culture during which the student seeks to apply what has been learned.

As a third value, I suggest that the right kind of experiential education constitutes a personal challenge, the meeting of which will produce outcomes which cannot be achieved very often through books, reports, lectures, discussions, and tests. These outcomes include an increased self-confidence, a deeper awareness of one's own strengths and weaknesses, and a heightened knowledge of effective approaches to other human beings—all of which come from having functioned successfully in a strange environment and under a different set of ground rules from those found in one's own culture. Not everyone can meet this challenge; perhaps not everyone should be expected to, a point to which I shall return in a moment. For those who adapt smoothly to lifestyles other than their own, however, there is a maturation which significantly transcends what is accomplished on the usual college or secondary school campus.

Fourth, I would list the holistic nature of experiential learning. Traditional education at the secondary and higher levels is becoming ever more specialized. But in an age of specialization we must not overlook the need for broad general understanding of the problems and issues that confront us. By functioning in a society, in addition to reading books and studying about it, we can more readily become aware of the interplay of forces—social, aesthetic, political, religious, economic—which comprise that society. I remember a young man in one of our programs whose assigned study in France was "The Impact of the Common Market on the French Bicycle Industry." He lived with the family of one of the union-shop stewards, spoke fluent French, worked part-time in the shipping department, interviewed such people as the plant manager (a Gaullist), the local priest (a radical Socialist), the *premier-adjoint* (highest assistant) in the town council (a Communist), and the editor of the local newspaper (a confirmed misogynist). He emerged with a heightened understanding of French culture and the place occupied within that culture by the bicycle industry. In other words, to switch for a moment to German, he grasped the *gestalt*.

As a fifth and final value—and one which obviously springs from all the others—I submit that experiential learning is soundly based upon what we know about how human beings best learn. John Dewey summed it up succinctly when he said, "Learn by doing." The Experiment in International Living adopted a parallel German saying, *Durch zusammenleben, lernt man zusammenleben*: "By living together, men and women learn to live together." I do not profess to be an educational psychologist, but in my thirty-six years in the field of education I have yet to be confronted with any firm evidence that denies this essential principle. It alone would justify all our efforts to provide more effective experiential educational opportunities.

I stress the words "more effective" because I have a fear that too many of us are satisfied simply to assume that any experience is a useful experience. To return for a moment to my French bicycle specialist, the effectiveness of his program came from careful planning and thoughtful use of the resources offered by the community of St. Étienne. He might have researched his paper by sitting in the bistro across the street from the Gitane plant and done a correlation study between the number of aperitifs he consumed and the increase in the number of bicycles he saw emerging from the plant. Experiential education demands a concentration on quality. It demands as well the consideration of a number of questions.

I go back to ancient Athens for a quote, "The unexamined life is not worth living" to introduce my first question: how do we examine and evaluate experiential learning? I am using the word "examine" in its broadest analytical sense. I do not suggest that all off-campus experiences must be followed by written examinations. In some fields, and I suggest foreign languages as being the most obvious, an examination, either oral or written, may be the easiest way to measure what has been learned during the experience. Such a test can measure correct use of verbs, knowledge of local idioms, vocabulary, and assorted other components. It cannot measure depth of knowledge and feeling about the culture in which the language is spoken. My question is a broad one: how can we measure the claimed outcomes of experiential education programs?

For a second question, I go back to the third value listed above, the personal maturation which comes from meeting and responding to the challenge of surviving an immersion in someone else's culture. Is cross-cultural educational experience something to which all students should be exposed, or are only certain ones qualified for it? I readily grant that there are various kinds of immersion, ranging from the quick dip in and out, through gentle floating on the surface with flippers and a breathing tube, to donning an scuba tank and exploring dangerously.

Are these levels sufficiently varied that all students can find their appropriate challenge? Should we establish academic prerequisites? Should only students with a 3.0 GPA or better be allowed off campus? What should be the basis on which students are enrolled in experiential programs?

One of my reasons for even suggesting selection standards is implicit in my third question: how much obligation do we assume toward the host culture in which these experiences are offered? When we enroll students in a laboratory course on campus, we are placing them in an educational setting which is completely under our control. When we encourage them to engage in experiential education, we are implicitly urging them to use a particular culture as their laboratory. Is this fair to the hosts? How would you and I react if a young Saudi Arabian, for example, were to visit our communities and our homes and ask us to assist him with a study in which he proposed to find out American attitudes toward cleanliness in public toilets? It is in many cases just such individual studies that we are inflicting upon our overseas hosts. Should there be a line drawn beyond which activity would be considered objectionable, intrusive? Who draws such a line, and how can it be justified to the student whose education will be inhibited thereby?

One final question may also be worth posing. In doing so I reiterate my earlier statement that affective education needs to be built upon a solid basis of cognitive knowledge. Is it possible to develop a set of equations or formulas which will reflect standards of balance between the two types of education we are here discussing? Does the junior year abroad—25 percent of a four-year undergraduate education—represent the ideal length? Is a semester of experiential education sufficient for most students? What about the institution which gives its students a few months on campus and then dispatches them overseas for the balance of a four-year program? Can we as educators establish appropriate proportions? Should we leave it to the students to decide where and in what way they assign their time?

I realize that in this presentation I have been guilty of narrowing the field of experiential education to that of cross-cultural activity, primarily in other nations. Having been guilty of thus circumscribing the field, let me close with a further transgression. On the basis of what I have said, I submit to you the following definition of "experiential education": it is a planned, affective, individual, thoughtfully evaluated component of an educational program. It will achieve its educational goals to the extent that it is characterized by these four adjectives.

3

Is Experiential Learning Something Fundamentally Different?

Theodore Gochenour

While the term may be a twentieth-century invention, "experiential learning" has been with us from the time one of our ancestors picked up a burning stick and thought better of it. Whether that ancestor had a name for the experience of pain or not, or whether he or she communicated to others with noises or gestures, something was learned.

Such learning still takes place among the normal hazards of growing up, but would not fall within what is usually dignified by the term "education." Yet the kind of learning called education is seen more and more to be arbitrarily limited—valuable in itself, but not the whole story. There has been a movement in the last half-century, initiated by John Dewey and aided by many since, to define, understand, and produce something called "experiential" education. Responding to pressures from students and faculty, colleges and universities have increasingly been interested in finding ways to accommodate to the growing sense that the means, goals, and assessments of traditional education are in need of a wider perspective.

Off-campus field experience, or experiential learning courses by whatever name, have become an increasingly recognized part of formal education. Broadly defined, these developments aim at emphasizing learning situations "in which the relative priority for effort is not upon work with symbols but with their referents: observing, interacting, performing, making things happen, feeling the effects of these activities and others' responses," to apply Keeton's useful distinction.[1] The schools and colleges involved in this educational direction have devoted considerable thought to matters such as how to issue credit, effective management of field-experience activities, and the identification of acceptable components making up experiential programs. Less successful have been efforts to develop a theoretical base which would clarify what is unique to experiential learning, what is actually learned experientially, or what might be worth learning. Questions such as what does experiential learning mean, how can it be measured, and what is it, remain unanswered in the background.

These questions are difficult to answer since they are themselves reflections of a cognitive, academic perspective. They assume that learning, thinking, and measuring are well understood and defined and that the problem is how to contain—or justify—experience-based learning within normal academic parameters. The answers may well lie outside these stated and implied perspectives. Suppose we were to assume that something very different is happening in experiential learning, that distinctly different mental processes are involved.

This assumption would require us to search for a basis which might clarify the intuitively felt differences between traditional classroom learning and experiential learning. It would imply a theoretical model sufficient to go beyond describing the operational effects, practical advantages, or academic issues involved in out-of-classroom programs. Such a theory should suggest avenues for not only examining whether any fundamental differences exist in the learning process itself, but also what implications such differences might have in measuring and assessing experiential education.

Human consciousness, particularly among the "third force" psychologies, has been returned to the central position it held many decades ago in the early years of the development of the field of psychology. Once we allow the behaviorists a place for their evidence that humans can be modified by external causes, we are still left with the realization—sensed inwardly by us all—that we are individual "selves," that we are identified in and by something called consciousness. This self, or consciousness, may be affected by outside events and causes, but it is nonetheless the observer of the external flow of forces and circumstances, and it acts continually though not always predictably.

If we acknowledge that consciousness as described here exists, it becomes important to understand the way it functions and its perceptual process. More specifically, we must consider that it functions in two contrasting modes of perceiving and thinking referred to variously as rational and intuitive or analytical and relational. Blessed or cursed as we may be by this ever present duality in our being, it has long ceased to be merely an interesting curiosity, inferred by observation, and has become the subject of accepted scientific study. Research into brain structure and the nature of consciousness indicates that we function through two contrasting modes of perceiving and thinking and that these bear a predictable relationship to the two halves of the human brain.

It follows that how and what we learn are profoundly affected by that same bimodal nature. We know there is a difference between learning to solve a math problem and the kind of learning which comes from life. Interestingly enough, we have learned of this difference the only way we can—through experience. The question here is whether the difference we recognize between experiential learning and academic learning relates in some way to our two modes of awareness and thinking. If it is valid to follow this line of approach, it may be possible to relate experiential learning to observable physical, neurological, and psychological properties of being human. It should be possible to know more clearly what experiential learning is or is not and how it relates to the better-known and clearly defined areas of cognitive learning.

Without attempting anything so grand as a theory of experiential learning, I suggest that a useful avenue of exploration lies in this fundamental fact of bimodal consciousness. To proceed, it is first necessary to understand something of what it is. Physically, our brains are divided into two hemispheres, each side capable of independent functioning, yet interconnected by fibrous tissue known as the "corpus callosum." The right side of the body is predominantly associated with the left hemisphere, and the left side of the body with the right hemisphere.

Both the structure and the function of these two "half brains" in some part underlie the two modes of consciousness which simultaneously coexist within each one of us. Although each hemisphere shares the potential for many functions and both sides participate in most activities, in the normal person the two hemispheres tend to specialize. The left hemisphere (which physiologically controls the right side of the body) is predominantly involved with analytic, logical thinking, especially in verbal and mathematical functions. Its mode of operation is primarily linear. This hemisphere seems to process information sequentially. This mode of operation of necessity must underlie logical thought, since logic depends on sequence and order. Language and mathematics, both left-hemisphere activities, also depend predominantly on linear time.

If the left hemisphere is specialized for analysis, the right hemisphere seems specialized for holistic mentation. Its language ability is quite limited. This hemisphere is primarily responsible for our orientation in space, for artistic endeavor, for intuition, nonverbal communication, and for such things as the recognition of faces. It processes information more diffusely than does the left hemisphere, and its responsibilities demand a ready integration of many inputs at once. If the left hemisphere can be termed predominantly analytic and sequential in its operation, then the right hemisphere is more holistic and relational and more simultaneous in its mode of operation.[2]

For over a century, evidence has accumulated to verify this bimodal view of consciousness, a scientific inquiry which appears to bear out our traditional, and culturally widespread, valuing of right and left. It is the right side of our bodies—and what the left hemisphere accomplishes—that we tend to value, and evidence for this is traceable in more than one language. That side is the verbal side, the side associated with that portion of the brain specializing in logical thinking, in naming, numbering, classifying, and analyzing—in short, with all that Western education traditionally identifies as worthwhile. Since the left hemisphere is the major seat of language, and our values usually only have meaning when they can be framed in words, people with strong left-hemisphere development enjoy a sort of "heads I win, tails you lose" monopoly. What is educationally valued is largely restricted to what can be conceptualized and put into words. The side which gives names to values is also the side which assigns meaning to those names. Our education is literally, then, one-sided.

It is important to remember, though, that our consciousness is not quite so readily split into neat categories. The urge to use such categories is itself an expression of only one part of us. Normally our functioning is a flowing process of alternation between the two modes, depending upon what we are engaged in. Most probably, it is a continuum in which both halves unite synergistically.

For purposes of clarity it may be useful to follow the path of classification and list some of the contrasting pairs of words which have been offered by many researchers to delineate these two modes:

RIGHT (Left Hemisphere)	LEFT (Right Hemisphere)
analytic	gestalt
lineal	nonlinear
sequential	simultaneous
verbal	spatial
intellectual	intuitive
differential	existential
rational	metaphoric
symbolic	visual/imaginative
discrete	diffuse
logical	synthetic, perceptual
propositional	appositional
numerical	geometric[3]

There may not be many ways of knowing and learning, but only two. Between these and in their interplay, we might find multiple nuances, but there appear to be two fundamental modes which can be broadly characterized, each linked to a side of the brain. We have a capacity for knowing and learning material which can be processed sequentially and conceptually; we seem equally to have a capacity for knowing and learning in holistic and existential ways. Though one mode has been linked historically with the process called education, and thereby given priority in value, we should not go to the opposite extreme and overvalue the metaphoric or appositional mode of consciousness.[4] It need not be a matter of crediting one and discrediting the other—essentially an absurdity—but of coming to the realization that both modes might best be allowed to function in synthesis harmoniously.

In applying this idea to education, we must realize that some kinds of learning cannot be pursued or given meaning through our verbal, rational side. Our tendency may be to grant the existence of bimodality in consciousness, yet cling to the habit of assigning meaning only as we are able to express it in words. A familiar case of this is the long tradition of "explaining" musical compositions. As the composer once said, while he played his work a second time in response to the question, What does it mean?—"It means **that**."

We would do well to understand that there are many kinds of knowing and learning for which we must find ways of valuing other than through concepts and words. While obviously any experience can in some way be put into cognitive terms, we should consider whether by so doing we have, in fact, explained anything. This especially applies to the whole area of experiential learning. All of us have had meaningful experiences which we sense mean more than the words available to describe them. Some of the difficulty students have with requirements to translate their experiential learning into intellectual terms can be understood in this light. If, in addition to our capacity for verbal, linear awareness, we have a capacity for existential, synthetic awareness, then we must grant that each of these two modes may have its own appropriate avenues of expression. To do otherwise may well provide no more than a bad translation—one seemingly satisfactory only because of the circular naming and valuing of the familiar, verbal mode.

All learning is an experience, thus experiential learning is something of a redundancy. Yet, for purposes of distinguishing between what has traditionally been defined as the educational process and that "other" for which a need is felt, the term may stand until replaced by one more descriptive. In essence, we commonly include in that term a range of hard-to-define processes which seem broadly to include the ways of knowing and learning associated with the metaphoric, spatial mode of our consciousness. It is simplistic to say that experiential learning is the functioning of that appositional mode. Yet it may be that we would find productive avenues for exploration in assuming a strong association to exist and thus freeing ourselves from the limitations of forcing all meanings and values to be expressible in cognitive terms.

For this approach we might define experiential learning (with apologies for being so abstract) as:

> that avenue to awareness and knowledge derived from the perception of existential wholes, causing change in the one experiencing them, expressible primarily in metaphoric, visual, imaginative, and spatial terms and, secondarily, in words and concepts.

If this definition can be provisionally accepted, it offers some clarification in looking at the terms often associated or identified with experiential learning. For example, it is important to avoid thinking that anything which happens outside the classroom is automatically experiential learning. Obviously, much of what comprises nonformal or field-experience education is well within the conceptual, linear, verbal, or numerical mode of traditional learning.

The approach to experiential learning proposed here is barely a start. Immediately we come to the awareness that it is much easier to describe the processes and count the honors of the conceptual side than of the other. The growth of science in the last few centuries can be seen as a special development in our propositional mode, along with the whole structure and content of our educational establishments. Due to the self-valuing properties of this mode, we lack the attention and the vocabulary with which to describe the achievements of our appositional side. Essentially we know much more of what one side is capable of than the other. The two modes of our consciousness seem to operate in essentially different, contrasting ways. The predominant capacities of one mode are either nonexistent or minimally functioning in the other. Neither mode is explainable in terms of the other, yet each provides a necessary increment to the total synthesis.

If we grant the existence of bimodality in consciousness, it is reasonable to allow it in learning. Can we go a step further and identify at least a few of the processes which may pertain specifically to experiential learning? We should be looking for situations requiring a capacity for spatial orientation; for artistic, manual, and athletic skills; for the direct apprehension of sense information without conceptual screens; for the activity of integrating lots of information simultaneously; for the shifting of a process from one at a time to a totally different sort of functioning, such as speed-reading. It goes without saying that there are undoubtedly many other processes going on here for which we presently do not have names.

It may be useful to recall that we are not looking for a set of processes in opposition to the cognitive, verbal ones, but complementary to them. At the same time we must avoid the tendency to decide how much such complementary processes are worth based on the degree to which they fit into a scale of analytical or numerical values. When one learns to play the piano, clearly the only meaningful evaluation is in the hearing. Since communication is one of the necessary and accepted objectives of education, it is appropriate to expect what is learned experientially to be communicable in some way. The important step is to distinguish which alternate kinds of communication or assessment might be appropriate in experiential learning and which kinds should be required to be translated into words. We should try to see the two modes in synthesis. Perhaps a useful initial realization is that we rarely, if ever, really think and learn by the linear, sequential models so often depicted. Though we may, after the fact, be able to give names to what seems like a logical process, our thinking in reality is a play between images and concepts and a synthetic combining process which seems to come from nowhere.

These ideas are offered as a possible theoretical base for further exploration and development of techniques. It is important to bear in mind that bipolarity in consciousness may be a neurological and psychological fact, but we need to refrain from a simplistic posture of either/or. There are, of course, a number of factors involved in experiential learning beyond those discussed here, among them: motivation; the relation of mind, emotions, and body; openness to learning; and self-awareness and self-management. Finally, it is useful to recognize the likelihood that the mind may function in still more complicated ways and that the mind and brain are not one and the same.

Notes:
1. Morris Keeton, "Cooperative Assessment of Experiential Learning Newsletter" 1, no.1 (July 1974).
2. Robert E. Ornstein, *The Psychology of Consciousness.* San Francisco: W. H. Freeman, 1972: 51-53.
3. Ornstein, 67. Also Joseph E. Bogen, "The Other Side of the Brain: An Appositional Mind." In *The Nature of Human Consciousness: A Book of Readings,* edited by Robert E. Ornstein. San Francisco: W. H. Freeman, 1973: 101-25.
4. Bogen, *op. cit.* Bogen proposed the word "appositional" as a term implying a capacity for the apposing or comparing of perceptions, schemes, engrams, etc., having in addition the virtue of implying very little else.

4

The Inner Side of Experiential Learning

Gordon Murray

I have directed programs in Nepal as a sort of unbridled learning experience, where students are encouraged to disregard the fences in which academic learning is often penned and let learning accompany them on whatever inner and outer adventures they pursue. I start with the assumption that everything they observe about Nepal is equally an observation about themselves and that every observation about themselves—their behaviors, feelings, values—likewise reflects Nepal. In this way I try to help them see their experiences not as exotic adventures but as integral parts of their lives, a chapter in their own broader evolution. I am often reinforced by the observation that when they feel good about that inner quest, they are more receptive to and involved in the outer world. Openness is openness, inner or outer.

What follows is a summary of my attempts to help people link cross-cultural learning with learning about themselves.

Stopping the World

A. THEORY

"You must realize that each man has a definite repertoire of roles which he plays in ordinary circumstances.... He has a role for every kind of circumstance in which he ordinarily finds himself in life; but put him into even only slightly different circumstances and he is unable to find a suitable role and for a short time he becomes himself."

For me the excitement of an experiential program has been participating in this process of "unbecoming" who we thought we were, experiencing the discomfort of being without familiar roles—stripped naked of our cultural clothing—and then in the vacuum thus created, "becoming ourselves": getting in touch with deeper, simpler, more fundamental human characteristics beneath our culture-bound personalities.

Though Nepali culture is the content of the learning here, it is not pinned down like a dead frog for dissection. It is as far as possible the living milieu in which the student carries out his or her real, total life for awhile. This is, in my understanding, the key distinction between purely academic learning and experiential learning. In the latter, the learner is more a part of the learned—it's all a big stew. So it seems valid to me to give equal attention to the inner world of the learner—values, concepts, roles—and the outer world of the learning environment—the Nepali culture. For it is at the interface of these two worlds where the exciting changes and growth are taking place.

B. PRACTICE: The Teacher As Model

Some time ago I gave a series of talks which attempted to provide an example of the kind of learning I thought could take place in the interface between me and Nepal. This exercise had several benefits. By sharing more of my life with the students, I became more of a real person to them. By showing how I had tried to embody my cross-cultural learning in my broader life, the learning became more concrete to the students and my learning model more credible. And the process of articulating my learning was a valuable exercise for me, giving me sustenance even as it contributed to the program.

I felt very good giving these talks. They were at once my single most valuable contribution to the program and my single most important self-learning experience. This coincidence strikes me as significant. When one puts energy into sharing what is important and challenging to one's own growth, chances are it will be valuable for other people's growth. The subject we know most about is ourselves, and the only real work we can do is on ourselves. Here is how Carlos Casteneda expresses it.

> Everyone who comes into contact with a child is a teacher who incessantly describes the world to him, until the moment when the child is capable of perceiving the world as it is described. According to Don Juan, we have no memory of that portentous moment, simply because none of us could possibly have had any point of reference to compare it to anything else. From that moment on, however, the child is a member. He knows the description of the world, and his membership becomes full-fledged, I suppose, when he is capable of making all the proper perceptual interpretations which, by conforming to that description, validate it.

> "You have simply stopped the world," he commented after I had finished my account.... "What was the thing that stopped in me?" "What stopped inside you yesterday was what people have been telling you the world is like. You see, people tell us from the time we are born that the world is such and such and so and so, and naturally we have no choice but to see the world the way people have been telling us it is."[1]

In Nepal, where we chose to come and live in the absence of so many familiar cultural cues, habitual behavior patterns that were once as comfortable as a pair of old faded jeans are suddenly stiff and starchy and out of place. Where once thank you and you're welcome punctuated our speech often and automatically, now there are no such words in the common vocabulary. Where once men and women walked casually arm in arm, now to touch in public brings stares of amazement. Where once the tender touch of one man to another was an anxiety-provoking sexual invitation, here men stroll lazily holding hands or sharing a bed in intimate but nonsexual affection. Where once we had a consistent "description of the world," as Don

Juan calls it, built up bit by bit since days past remembering, resulting in a complex world of semiconscious habitual reactions and behaviors, now we are stripped bare; we have "stopped the world."

The mind puts up a strong resistance to being thus deprived of its reality patterns. It throws up fear and value judgment and projection—what we call "culture shock"—in repeated attempts to defend its threatened security. Gradually, as it learns the "description of the world" of the new culture, it loosens its hold on the old description. And at times a gap opens between the two descriptions, where the mind glimpses the highly conditioned nature every minute of its operation and, at once horrified and liberated, feels a deeply releasing sense of openness, space, and tolerance.

People experience this in their own particular ways. To illustrate, I want to share some of the ways my description of the world was "stopped" in Nepal and some of the ways I've tried to integrate my experiences into a new description of the world. I'll take as a general description of who I was when I first went to Nepal the sentence "I am a middle-class American male" and touch on how the four parts of this description have changed over the years.

1. "Male": Sex-Role Conditioning

I grew up in an atmosphere where sex was never discussed. There was a subtle but definite message that sex was somehow a preoccupation of vulgar people. The highest pleasures were the pleasures of the mind. Physical sensations were ignored to the point that the mind could almost forget it dwelled in this inconvenient form called a body. Mind and body were assumed to be fundamentally dissimilar. To suggest a connection bordered on a sort of bodily socialism— a corporal analogy to class-leveling—and was therefore heretical.

My information on sex and sex roles came not through open discussion but through films, advertising, jokes, and the kind of indirect sexual jousting and social banter which never come directly and naturally to the point, but only indicate by innuendo and implication the proper roles of men and women. And, of course, there were the tacit and powerful sex-role models of my parents. Information gathered in these ways gradually crystallized into stereotypical images of men and women. Males were strong, dominant, competent. With other males they were competitive, powerful, even aggressive. Humor was appropriate but tenderness and weakness were not. The rational side was acceptable but the feeling and intuitive sides were not. With females, men could reveal their vulnerability and allow women to mother them and provide emotional support as long as it never threatened their ultimate power or command over the relationship. By contrast, in the world in which I grew up, women were weak, submissive, emotional, irrational. They had a monopoly on feeling and intuition. They were the comforters, the nurturers, the source of warm tenderness. They were protected by the hard shell of the male from the roughness of what was rightly described as "a man's world" in which they were naturally too weak to participate. Theirs was the proverbial "women's work" which was never done: the cyclical tasks of cooking, cleaning, and nurturing the growing offspring. Homosexual men—though of course no one actually knew any—were thought of as effeminate women haters; homosexual women—why, they didn't even exist. This was my sexual description of the world.

One evening in Nepal I was listening to the nightly recitation from the holy books at a friend's house when it began to rain. My friend said I should spend the night there, so I took my place on the floor alongside the several brothers of the family. In the middle of the night my friend threw his arms around me and kissed me, saying "This is Nepali love." In the morning the world had a different feel to it.

The taboo against males showing physical affection to one another is strong in our culture. In Nepal a relaxed physical affection among male friends is the norm, a facet of the Nepali description of the world.

From my stopping of the world in Nepal, I gradually came to acknowledge that I felt physical attraction for men and began to express that. I found that learning to act on gay feelings was learning to get in touch with my body, for there were no models other than my feelings to go by. The only model for such relationships offered by our culture until recently was an exaggerated stereotype of homosexual, which felt as foreign to my own nature as did the stereotypic macho male. By learning to base my physical relations with people on inner feelings rather than outward, culture-bound expectations and images and to relate to people, rather than males or females, I began to feel more comfortable and natural with both sexes. A new description of the world started developing which continues to this day.

2. "Middle Class": Economic Class Conditioning

Perhaps one of the reasons it was important for middle-class people to ignore sex with such puritanical rigor was that sex tended to distract from the really important task in life: upward mobility. Sex was not only vulgar, it was cheap and, somehow, the province of the lower classes. The economic and sexual descriptions of the world fit together like a jigsaw puzzle: there was a sexually indulgent, economically stagnant lower class; a sexually stagnant, economically indulgent middle class; and rumors of an upper class—movie stars and other bigwigs—who could afford to be both sexually and economically indulgent.

The drive for upward mobility was rooted in the very real sufferings of being poor, especially during the Depression, which showed that one could never climb high enough on the ladder of success to be totally safe from the demon Poverty. This was all part of my upbringing and part of the urgency behind the familiar refrain, "What do you want to be when you grow up?"

This last question bears some analysis. First of all, the answer is invariably given in terms of economic role rather than characteristics or qualities: I want to be a doctor, lawyer, merchant, or thief—not I want to be kind or skillful or well-rounded or perceptive. Furthermore, the verb "to grow up" shares the subliminal sense of finality or completion pointed out by Benjamin Lee Whorf, common to all verbs suffixed with "up": to clean up, sweep up, eat up, lock up. Grownups, then, are people who have stopped growing; they've arrived. Where? At some economic niche whose security must not be threatened by further growth, experiment, adventure, openness, or change. This is the dubious model of the proper life implied in the seemingly harmless question, "What do you want to be when you grow up?"

In a traditional Nepali village there is no notion of upward mobility. People live in the way of their ancestors since time began—farming—and farming in a particular way which has evolved slowly, imperceptibly over the generations. These people live so far below the poverty line and the various minimum daily requirements that those measurements simply lose their sense. They live, as I did for a time, without electricity, running water, and other so-called necessities of life. Yet as I lived among them I noticed they did not seem substantially less happy, less fulfilled, or less sane on account of their poverty. I began to reflect that the correlation between happiness and economic progress was tenuous and misleading at best.

The experience of living in a simple Nepali style was a stopping of my economic world. Since then my description of the world has had a new set of economic assumptions. Simple living—taking care of my material needs without leading a highly consuming, wasteful, indulgent economic life and without needing to judge my value as a person in economic terms—makes sense to me.

Finally, I assume that I will never grow "up"—never stop growing. A plant sprouts, flowers, goes to seed, withers, dies. How am I different from a flower? I believe that it was Carl Rogers who said that he felt he changed as much from sixty-five to seventy-five as during any previous decade of his life, and why not? I hope to remain useful and growing until I die. I choose to trust in the process of my life, though it be a winding path invisible beyond the next bend, rather than choose the visible but deadening security of becoming grown-up.

3. "American": Cultural Conditioning

This is such a broad area that I want to focus on just one narrow but significant aspect—our sense of self—and contrast that with a very different sense of self which I encountered in Nepal.

Perhaps our sense of self is rooted in shared archetypes of bold pilgrims and pioneers and a frontier struggle which favored rugged individualists. Our history as a nation begins with individuals trying to gain power over their own lives by getting out from under the tyranny of groups, and the theme of respect for individuals and mistrust of groups still runs strong in our conditioning. From an early age we are taught about private property: it's my toy and not yours, my room and no one else's.

Learning to read strengthens this archetypical and childhood emphasis on the individual. A major theme of Marshall McLuhan's *Understanding Media*[2] is how the experience of literacy has the subliminal effect of etching into the mind a profound sense of self as distinct from the group. Reading is fundamentally a private act; one must go out of one's way to make it public by reading aloud.

Otherwise, the act of reading adds to my own private stock of experience. Even if you and I read the same book, our experience is more private than, say, if we attend the same poetry reading. The sense of my own unique self with its special store of knowledge is developed to great depths in the literate person.

Other important subliminal consequences of literacy, according to McLuhan, include linear logic and a linear sense of time. The fact that a book is really one long line of information—broken up for convenience into lines and pages—conveys the subliminal message that knowledge can, in fact, be expressed linearly. For the literate person, it makes sense to analyze the world by a "train" of thought, a "line" of argument, a "series" of deductions—what we call "logic." Furthermore, the fact that words are made up of arbitrary phonetic signs having no independent meaning predisposes our minds to accept a sense of time made up of arbitrary uniform segments having no experiential meaning. That is, we don't tell time in terms of feelings like readiness, boredom, anxiousness, but by seconds, minutes, and hours which have no correlates in nature. That we have invested these abstract units of time with a concrete substance and reality wholly independent of our experiences in time is reflected in our vocabulary: "Time is money," so we must "spend" it wisely and avoid "wasting" it. Of course time "flies" and, occasionally, when we "kill" it, even dies.

This highly developed sense of individual self, with its notions of private property and space, its linear logic and notion of abstract time, becomes clear in contrast to what McLuhan calls "oral" cultures, of which Nepal is a good example. The archetypical unit here is the group, not the individual. From an early age children are taught to think of themselves as intimately bound to a series of concentric groups—extended family, village, caste—which are in turn rigidly distinguished from other groups of the same type. The smallest property-holding unit is not the individual, but the extended family, the use of possessions being determined by consulting the male hierarchy: younger brother obeys elder, son obeys father, wife obeys husband. Even a person's name often reflects the group. Last names are most often caste names, and the young are very often called by their rank in the family, e.g., "second son" or "youngest daughter," rather than by their given name.

In oral cultures like Nepal, the bulk of the transfer of information comes through oral interactions with people rather than through the printed page. In contrast to the inherently private written medium, the oral medium is intrinsically public; one must go out of one's way to make it private by retreating out of earshot. Thus the sense of identity with the group is strengthened; the stock of private experience is not built up to anywhere near the extent it is in a literate person.

Similarly, no sense of linear logic is developed in an oral culture. The logic of conversation is filled with characteristics the literate person calls "illogical": emotion, digression, redundancy. The syllogisms of oral logic are made up not of premise, argument, and conclusion, or of necessary and sufficient conditions, but rather of a complex test of sincerity and intensity of feeling in which repetition and a loud voice are valid tools. Finally, the sense of time in an oral culture tends to be based on natural cycles, hence is experiential and cyclical rather than abstract and linear. The seasons repeat endlessly; each year rice is planted in the same way it always has been; time is made up of experiential repetition and moments of varying intensity, rather than an infinite line of abstract units marching ever onward.

In my experience in Nepal, countless little characteristics which seemed mysterious or irritating or absurd when viewed through my American description of the world were made clear by McLuhan's analysis of the oral culture's description of the world. For example, in a Nepali home there is a lack of private space. People sleep together, children are rarely excluded from adult conversations or gatherings, there are fewer doors. A family member is apt to pop in and stare at the strange new Westerner at great length, without thinking twice about it. Nor is property private. One's possessions are apt to be methodically examined, unbidden, with frequent requests that things be given away. After all, if the foreigner is a "member" of the family, the property must also be the family's. Explanations for all sorts of behaviors will be given unself-consciously in terms of groups: "Brahmins don't eat pork," "We do it this way," "This is Nepali love."

Then, the Nepali sense of time: If an event is called for 6:00 P.M. but doesn't start until 8:00 P.M., no one minds except the American, for whom the abstract meaningless units have been ticking away with maddening relentlessness for two whole hours. For the Nepali of prewristwatch technology, the smallest unit of time is a quarter-day: there is morning, daytime, evening, and night. Time is measured more experientially and concretely, filled out with the reality of feeling. If things aren't ready by 6:00 P.M., it's not that they are late; it simply isn't time to begin yet.

With respect to individuality, thought patterns, space, and time, the Westerner living in an oral culture is constantly interacting with a people whose description of the world is vastly different. If his or her own cultural conditioning continues to interpret behaviors in terms of its own description, frustration and misunderstanding result. Only when the person can relax that description and stop the world do things fall into clear and sensible patterns.

4. "I": Ego Conditioning

"Who are you?" said the caterpillar.... Alice replied rather shyly, "I—I hardly know, sir, just at present—at least I know who I was when I got up this morning, but I think I must have been changed several times since then."

Lewis Carroll, *Alice's Adventures in Wonderland*

Buddhist psychology offers a model to get at the deepest roots of our conditioning: the notion of a permanent "I" or ego. Whether I've grown up with a highly literate, Western notion of "I" as a distinct individual or an oral culture's description of numerous "we's" with which I identify, there is the tendency to believe in something permanent underlying all my experiences. This sense of a permanent ego is an illusion, according to the Buddhists: we have been exposed to a series of descriptions of the world that have all been couched in terms of "I" since time-out-of-memory, which has led us to the blind conclusion that an "I" exists, independent of the ever changing perceptual flow of our experience. Buddhist psychology, on the other hand, views the "I" as more fluid and distinguishes twelve stages or consequences of ego conditioning. In the Tibetan tradition, these stages are depicted on the Wheel of Life, which is a sort of layperson's pictorial summary of the main Buddhist principles, painted at the entrance of most Tibetan temples.

There is no "I"; there is only the flow. We are like a beaver building a dam: we take bits and pieces out of the flow of the river of our experience and tangle them together into a whole which is greater than the sum of its parts—the dam. The dam successfully blocks the river, creating a still, calm pool called "I" in which we can function. The problem is that we tend to forget that the pool is impermanent, that the dam is only a temporary arrangement of pieces taken from a much more fundamental flow.

This Buddhist perspective seems to me an especially healthy one for the stranger in a strange land—the foreigner in another culture. To be open to and observant of both the inner and outer flow, without reacting, judging, evaluating: this is the first step, is it not, to understanding ourselves and the culture? It is a mechanism for stopping the world. By watching our own feelings and perceptions, noting our tendencies to react with grasping and craving or dislike and aversion, we watch in intimate detail the process by which we have built up our beaver dam—our most basic description of the world—our notion of "I." By stopping that buildup of habitual responses, we open the space for new reactions to occur, the space of openness, change, growth, and learning.

That reminds me of the Zen story of the pupil who came to tea at the master's. The master was serving the tea and filled the pupil's cup and kept on pouring so the tea ran out onto the floor. Finally, the pupil could no longer stand it and burst out, "Enough! The cup is more than full!" The master replied, "The cup is like your mind: so full that there is no more room. If you are to learn anything, first you must be empty of what you already know."

Integration: Getting It Together

"Le coeur a ses raisons que la raison ne connait point."
Blaise Pascal, *Pensées*

A. THEORY

Head and heart: one of those good old eternal dichotomies. Pick your flavor: Pascal's dichotomy between reason and heart; the Greek distinction between the cool, rational, ordered Apollonian mode and the frenzied, emotional, unrestrained Dionysian; Hesse's recurring dialogue between the rational, scholarly, intellectual side (Narcissus) and the emotional, artistic, feeling side (Goldmund)[3]; or the contemporary researcher's discovery of the linear, logical, analytic left brain and the nonlinear, symbolic, synthetic right brain. Whatever metaphor you choose, it seems safe to say that polar tendencies exist within the human potential.

Much commotion has arisen over the fact that our educational establishment emphasizes largely the analytic, intellectual left-brain half of this dichotomy to the exclusion of synthetic, feeling, right-brain learning and growth. In Nepal—and I suspect in any cross-cultural setting—there is a great opportunity to redress the balance.

B. PRACTICE

1. Choosing a Project: "Where Are You At?"

Here are some examples of independent study projects in Nepal which have provided students with the chance to integrate their experiences in Nepal with their own lives and personal development.

Susan (all these names will be fictitious) had decided to do a project on "Women in Nepal" but had gotten stuck. She had adequate resources and ideas, but for some reason had lost all her enthusiasm. We discussed what was really happening in her life: ambiguous feelings about her highly intellectual and competitive college life; about the people in her life—parents, brother, boyfriend; and, at the core of it all, about herself. I suggested that she might try centering her project on herself: her womanhood, her own conditioning, her own roles. Blocked energy began to flow. She wrote a lengthy autobiography, using the perspective afforded by being in Nepal to connect her head—notions of womanhood, roles, and cultural conditioning —with her heart, the struggles of her real life.

George was doing a project on Tibetan spiritual practice, but like Susan, had lost enthusiasm and drive amidst plentiful resources. We discussed, again, what was really preoccupying him. He was having trouble reconciling an outward study of Buddhism with his inward spiritual practice of five years. I suggested he reverse the emphasis—place his own spiritual path at the center of the project and let the Tibetan environment stimulate a new perspective. The shift of emphasis worked; he found new energy by integrating his head—

observations about the Tibetan way—with his heart, his own spiritual path.

These two examples were so striking in their similarity and simplicity that I learned a formula for unsticking a stuck project. Detach yourself a moment and give yourself permission to ask what is really on your mind, preoccupying you, blocking or taking up your energy—where your heart is at. Then put that at the center of your project and let your head integrate in and around your heart.

2. Making Connections: "A Path with a Heart"

Successful independent-study projects almost always make this kind of connection between head and heart or, more broadly speaking, between a person's intellectual interests and the requirements of his or her school, on the one hand, and the person's broader life and nonintellectual side. Projects which are not fueled by the whole person quickly stagnate and dry up in the absence of the familiar pressures of classrooms, teachers, tests, and peer momentum. Here are some more examples.

Randy had said on the very first day of orientation that a goal of his was to learn to listen better. He ended up doing his project on a Tibetan monastery which involved long hours spent simply listening to chanting. Consciously or unconsciously, he had arranged for a project which demanded many hours of pure listening, a skill he could later apply to other contexts in his broader life.

Scott was deeply distressed with his overintellectual life and wanted to learn other ways of being. He did a project on the economics of a Tibetan refugee center whose main source of income was a carpet factory. His research involved long hours sitting in the factory weaving his own carpet—learning to use his hands and letting his mind feel the rhythm of his subject matter in a whole new way. When he was done, he had plenty of material on the economics of carpet weaving, plus a carpet he'd woven, plus the beginnings of an exploration into some nonintellectual parts of himself.

Alice was timid and had a hard time talking to people. She designed a project that involved dozens of interviews which demanded that she encounter new people and take some personal risks, but within the relative safety of the structured interview. Thus she combined a personal-growth goal with a scholarly one.

Elizabeth had never felt comfortable playing hostess—it was an awkward role for a liberated woman and Doris Lessing fan. But she wanted to be able to be hospitable. She designed a project on Sherpa hospitality. Sherpa hospitality is both an elaborate and a prominent characteristic of the culture and provided Elizabeth with a great deal of material for good scholarly fieldwork. It also touched on a personal concern of hers, offering a fresh way of looking at her own attitudes toward hospitality.

Successful projects integrate the past with the present, the home culture with the new culture, the head with the heart, the demands of academe with "where you're at." A successful project is always, in Don Juan's words, "a path with a heart."

3. Souvenirs: "Bringing It All Back Home"

Finally comes time for perhaps the most difficult integration: going home. How to bring this exotic dream stuff back to all those folks at home who will ask, "What was it like?" In a basic way, of course, the underlying theme of this article—the integration of inner and outer learning—makes this transition easier, for one carries around inner learnings without suitcases, slides, or postcards. If one keeps in mind that these inner souvenirs are the really significant ones, then communicating with the folks back home becomes easier.

I inherited from a friend a useful transition exercise for ending the program. I walk the students through the entire three-month experience, from the day they packed up and left home to the present moment, stopping at a dozen or so significant points along the way: the first day of homestay, a moment in trekking, and so on. I tell them to get in touch with a feeling from that moment and write it down in one or two words. They are left with a list of a dozen or so significant feelings—excitement, terror, loneliness, awe, boredom, bravery, pain, hilariousness—each one a sort of chapter heading serving to recall a whole bunch of stories, incidents, and other feelings. By expressing these feelings to the person to whom they are trying to convey their Nepal experience, they will likely trigger that person to share some of his or her own experiences under that same "chapter heading." The language of feeling is universal and transports easily from culture to culture. I can bore you to death describing the interior of a Hindu home, but if I describe my feelings of terror and discomfort there, chances are you'll respond.

Conclusion: The Paradox

This article has made a case for paying attention to the inner learning afforded by living in a cross-cultural environment. The paradox of going to another culture to understand oneself is nicely expressed by Heinrich Zimmer in his *Myths and Symbols in Indian Art and Civilization*, and I'd like to close with this wonderful tale.

> It is a brief story, told of the Rabbi Eisik, son of Rabbi Jekel, who lived in the ghetto of Cracow, the capital of Poland. He had remained unbroken in his faith, through years of affliction, and was a pious servant of the Lord his God.
>
> One night, as this pious and faithful Rabbi Eisik slept, he had a dream: the dream enjoined him to proceed, afar, to the Bohemian capital, Prague, where he should discover a hidden treasure buried beneath the principal bridge leading to the castle of the Bohemian kings. The Rabbi was surprised and put off his going. But the dream recurred twice again. After the third call, he bravely girded his loins and set forth on the quest.
>
> Arriving at the city of his destiny, Rabbi Eisik discovered sentries at the bridge, and these guarded it day and night, so that he did not venture to dig. He only returned every morning and loitered around until dusk, looking at the bridge, watching the sentries, studying unostentatiously the masonry and the soil. At length, the captain of the guards, struck by the old man's persistence, approached and gently inquired whether he had lost something or perhaps was waiting for someone to arrive. Rabbi Eisik recounted, simply and confidently, the dream that he had had, and the officer stood back and laughed.
>
> "Really, you poor fellow!" the captain said, "Have you worn your shoes out wandering all this way only because of a dream? What sensible person would trust a dream? Why look, if I had been one to go trusting dreams, I should this very minute be doing just the opposite. I should have made just such a pilgrimage as this silly one of yours, only in the opposite direction, but no doubt with the same result. Let me tell you my dream."

He was a sympathetic officer, for all of his fierce mustache, and the Rabbi felt his heart warm to him. "I dreamt of a voice," said the Bohemian Christian officer of the guard, "and it spoke to me of Cracow, commanding me to go thither and to search there for a great treasure in the house of a Jewish rabbi whose name would be Eisik son of Jekel. The treasure was to have been discovered buried in the dirty corner behind the stove. Eisik son of Jekel!" The captain laughed again, with brilliant eyes. "Fancy going to Cracow and pulling down the walls of every house in the ghetto, where half of the men are called Eisik and the other half Jekel! Eisik son of Jekel, indeed!" And he laughed, and he laughed again at the wonderful joke.

The unostentatious Rabbi listened eagerly, and then, having bowed deeply and thanked his stranger-friend, he hurried straightway back to his distant home, dug in the neglected corner of his house and discovered the treasure which put an end to all his misery. With a portion of the money he erected a prayer-house that bears his name to this day.

Now the real treasure, to end our misery and trials, is never far away; it is not to be sought in any distant region; it lies buried in the innermost recess of our own home, that is to say, our own being. And it lies behind the stove, the life-and-warmth-giving center of the structure of our existence, our heart of hearts—if we could only dig. But there is an odd and persistent fact that it is only after a faithful journey to a distant region, a foreign country, a strange land, that the meaning of the inner voice that is to guide our quest can be revealed to us. And together with this odd and persistent fact there goes another, namely, that the one who reveals to us the meaning of our cryptic inner message must be a stranger, of another creed and a foreign race.[4]

Notes:

1. Carlos Casteneda. *Journey to Ixtlan* (New York: Simon & Schuster, 1972) 9, 299. Casteneda presents an interesting and useful idea in this case, whatever the merits may otherwise be of his work. (The Editor.)

2. Marshall McLuhan. *Understanding Media: The Extensions of Man* (New York: New American Library, 1964).
3. Hermann Hesse's *Narcissus and Goldmund* is a novel of two medieval men who embody the conflict between flesh and spirit, between emotional and contemplative approaches to life.
4. Heinrich Zimmer, *Myths and Symbols in Indian Art and Civilization.* Edited by Joseph Campbell (New York: Pantheon Books, 1946).

For a more detailed account of an independent-study program in South Asia similar to the one on which this article is based, see Jennifer Ladd, *Subject India: A Semester Abroad* (Yarmouth, ME: Intercultural Press, 1990).

5

Focus on Process: An Examination of the Learning and Teaching of Intercultural Communicative Competence*

Alvino E. Fantini

In his book, *25 Centuries of Language Teaching* (1969), Louis Kelly demonstrates dramatically that there is little new today in the teaching of languages that was not already known or tried centuries ago. In fact, the teaching profession is continuously in the habit of reinventing the wheel, restating premises, and seeking a new direction every few years, always with renewed enthusiasm as though "the way" to second-language teaching had finally been discovered.

In more recent years, through the combined efforts of psychologists and linguists, there have been increasing attempts to couple psychological theories of learning with advances in linguistics. This

---

*For a discussion of how some of the concepts examined in this chapter are applied in instructional situations, see another article by Fantini in this volume, "Language and Intercultural Orientation: A Process Approach."

psycholinguistic approach has itself created several new pedagogical viewpoints, or methods, of language teaching. The problem, however, is that too often certain viewpoints have been adopted to the exclusion of others. Narrow theoretical perspectives became embodied in methods based on a limited number of ways in which human beings learn. Psychological theories have been exclusive, rather than inclusive, in scope. Within linguistics, theories have been equally exclusive, resulting in only partial or inadequate explanations of language learning.

Examples of exclusivist approaches in psychological learning theory or linguistics are not hard to find. For example, within linguistics a major debate has existed for over a decade between structural analysis and transformationalism. Within psychology, disagreement has occurred between behaviorist and cognitive viewpoints. Yet it is becoming increasingly clear that the issue is not one of either/or, but rather of a need to expand theory to accommodate the differing viewpoints. Structuralism and transformationalism, for example, each focus on a distinct aspect of language. Whereas structuralists analyze the surface of an utterance, transformationalists seek to uncover the underlying generative rules responsible for producing that utterance. In each case, however, the analysis is only a partial one.

Another development which has begun to force linguists to consider both "competence" (the underlying knowledge of a speaker) and "performance" (the actual act of speaking) is the convincing research being done by sociolinguists. Sociolinguists have brought to our attention the fact that the dichotomy between competence and performance is quite artificial and that their interrelationship must be accounted for in any explanation of language. That is, one cannot write a complete grammar if the *use* of language in its social context is ignored. Most sociolinguists would agree that transformationalists have only examined language technology (its construction), whereas what must concern us are the broader aspects of communicative competence, of which the utterance is only part. Furthermore, the form of language—the technological construct—follows function and not the reverse, which has been the view held for so long.

In addition, one examines the variations of linguistic form in relation to the social context in which they are used. As one realizes that all speakers everywhere and at all times control not one stable, immutable form of speech, but rather numerous styles, each consistent with a specific set of social circumstances, it becomes clear that language cannot be viewed as abstract knowledge unrelated to social context. Likewise, if one denies social context as an important determinant of linguistic choice, then one cannot account for other aspects of human interaction, which indeed also serve to communicate, sometimes even contradicting, what is expressed through words. Most paralinguistic aspects of communication cannot be accounted for if we limit ourselves to generative rules for verbal language without consideration of the total scope of communicative acts.

Mackey alludes to the fragmentation of theoretical viewpoints when he talks of bilingualism and second-language learning:

> Bilingualism (and other aspects of second language acquisition, I might add), cannot be described within the science of linguistics; we must go beyond. Linguistics has been interested in bilingualism only insofar as it could be used as an explanation for changes in a language, since language, not the individual, is the proper concern of this science. Psychology has regarded bilingualism as an influence on mental processes. Sociology has treated bilingualism as an element in culture conflict. Pedagogy has been concerned with bilingualism in connection with school organization and media of instruction. For each of these disciplines bilingualism is incidental, it is treated as a special case or as an exception to the norm. Each discipline, pursuing its own particular interests in its own special way.... But it seems to add little to our understanding of bilingualism as such, with its complex psychological, linguistic, and social interrelationships.

What is needed, to begin with, is a perspective in which these interrelationships may be considered (Mackey 1970, 554).

With this in mind, it should be clear that pedagogy suffers direct consequences of the incompleteness of both psychological learning theories and linguistic analyses. Most methods are directly constructed on selected biases, which assume that human beings learn in one specific way or another, failing to recognize that humans learn in a variety of ways beyond the scope of the chosen theory. This results in the built-in narrowness of our teaching methods and controversies between those who have aligned themselves with one method or another.

It appears that each individual uses various strategies to learn, in varying combinations, at different times. Consequently, a more logical approach would appear to be one which recognizes all of the strategies which psychologists have identified as those used by human beings in the learning process. Where then does this leave the teacher who has relied on a method constructed on only a few of these strategies?

Herein lies the origin of numerous problems in the teaching profession. One method after another has, in fact, appeared not only over the past two decades, but over the past two thousand years. Teachers are too often staunchly in favor of, or in opposition to, one or another of them. Methods have arisen, each with a following of practitioners, only to fall into disrepute a few years later. Often with the disappearance of each method, the profession almost begins anew as it throws out the proverbial baby with the bathwater. This is the case described in Kelly's history of language teaching in which he relates how the Greeks, Comenius, Saint Augustine, the grammarians of the seventeenth century, the traditionalists, the followers of the direct method, the audiolingual approach, and more recently the supporters of cognitive-code learning each discarded what preceded in order to implement a newer method (Kelly 1969).

As one becomes aware of the historical development of methodology, the question arises: How can it be that after two thousand years there is still so much controversy among those concerned with the same problem, the same issues, and normally with the same dedication? How can there be so much inconsistency and doubt in the profession after two thousand years of accumulated knowledge? Is it not possible that there is some value in each of the methods that are theoretically and pragmatically developed? Would there not be some value in salvaging all that is worthwhile, incorporating this into a harmonious whole? How can we synthesize what is known into a framework which will permit diverse methods of language teaching to coexist within one broad perspective?

Such a synthesis is the subject of this paper. What is proposed here is a framework in which the apparent inconsistencies of differing methods may be resolved. The title "Focus on Process" has been chosen for this framework since the emphasis is on process. To understand the process approach, we must first clarify the terms "technique," "method," and "approach." These terms are often used indiscriminately and interchangeably; however, a more precise usage is essential. A technique is a specific learning activity designed to achieve an immediate learning objective. A method is generally a combination of selected techniques, often chosen according to how they fit certain theoretical assumptions. An approach is much broader in scope and commonly encompasses various techniques and methods. In addition, an approach usually permits considerably more latitude than a method in that it is based on broader, and sometimes less clearly articulated, theoretical assumptions.

Having created this hierarchy of terminology, it is the author's contention that we must immediately forego addiction to any one method. This is essential since, as has been pointed out, each method has an implicit, theoretical assumption (usually too limiting) on which it is constructed. Furthermore, a method generally implies distinct behavioral parameters which often result in a series of do's and don't's. As we speak of methods—whether method X or Y—we begin to discover that there are often areas of overlap, but even more often direct contradictions or inconsistencies. Method X or Y translated into a teacher's handbook normally results in guidelines which may be controversial. Teachers often find that such guidelines impinge upon the realities they have known in the classroom and/or are incompatible with their own teaching style or the students' learning styles. Consequently, effective teachers learn to meander back and forth across the limits imposed by a number of methods, even when they ostensibly favor a particular one. Yet knowing that they are not following a method in the pure sense sometimes produces an uneasy, guilt-ridden feeling. Although they are doing something which pragmatically works, they are uneasy in the knowledge that a given activity may be theoretically inconsistent with the chosen method. Such guilt surfaces most noticeably when a supervisor appears, in which case the teacher reverts immediately to a stricter adherence to "method."

Although many teachers may begin with a particular method, they become increasingly eclectic with experience. Experienced teachers are more prone to react if subjected to the limitations of method. If permitted, experienced teachers commonly reject any text or method which demands too strict adherence, preferring the latitude to teach in accordance with their own abilities, personalities, and interests as well as those of their students.

The famed Pennsylvania Project, conducted over a period of three years and costing over $300,000, purportedly set out to compare the results of the traditional grammar-translation method of language teaching with the audiolingual method, as well as the effects of audio materials on students. One of the striking aspects of the study was that although teachers were assigned (or volunteered) to teach in one of the methods, it was discovered that most teachers combined teaching activities from both (Smith 1970).

Most teachers are continually developing their own techniques to facilitate learning as they gain experience. These techniques may or may not be associated with a particular method. It would be impossible to compile an exhaustive list of these techniques. Yet with so many possibilities, one wonders how a teacher decides which technique to pull out of an unlimited bag of tricks. Certain techniques may be more effective than others for particular aspects of learning, at particular stages of learning, and with particular students. What is needed, then, is a framework which will help one make an appropriate choice of one technique or another in each context. The process approach provides one possible framework.

Basically, a process approach focuses on the language-development process, identifying prominent stages of learning. It is based on the understanding that:

1. People learn in a variety of ways. Furthermore, individual learners vary the strategies they use in accordance with a variety of factors present at the moment. Although most learners are unaware of when and which strategy is being used, nonetheless they know when they are learning and when they are confused, which is one clue as to what works and what does not.

2. All techniques available to teachers must have some value, regardless of the method from which each is derived. Because all techniques have some potential value—especially when used within an appropriate context—we should be careful not to exclude any.

3. Each student has a distinct personality, competence, and other attributes, as does each teacher. Because of this, an approach should permit the teacher—in conjunction with the learner— freedom to consider all of this in selecting techniques appropriate to a given situation.
4. Finally, although all techniques have some value, there should be some rationale which guides selection rather than a random choice from a vast armory of techniques (based on what is known about learning theory, linguistic theory, the teacher, the learner, and the available techniques).

Hence, a process approach to language teaching and learning seeks the broadest possible perspective of teaching and learning— one which includes rather than excludes all that is known and available. It encourages optimum matching of student, context, pedagogical approach, and teacher. The focus is on the student and the development process, but the realities of the teacher's own abilities within a given context are not ignored.

A process approach first identifies several stages which lead toward the development of intercultural communicative competence. These are:

1. Presentation of, or exposure to, new material
2. Practice with this material in limited contexts
3. Explanation/elucidation of the material where necessary or useful
4. Transposition of the material (in combination with other material already learned by the student) into freer contexts and more spontaneous conversation
5. Sociolinguistic exploration of the interrelationship of language and the social context, emphasizing the appropriateness of language use (in addition to its grammatical correctness)
6. Cultural exploration as the basis for interactional strategy
7. Intercultural exploration by comparing and contrasting the target culture with the learner's native culture

The first four stages are probably already familiar to most language teachers. The last three, however, are often beyond the purview of what is considered to be the subject matter of language teaching. Although stage one may be an obvious starting point,

stages two and three are easily interchangeable. Such interchange-
ability bypasses the old debate among educators as to whether
learning is best served through an inductive or deductive approach.
Have we not all discovered that it has sometimes made just as much
sense to approach a problem inductively as it has deductively? Some
teachers favor explanation followed by practice; others prefer practice followed by explanation, and often the same teacher will vary
these. Whether or not we agree, we can at least permit the flexibility
to interchange these steps for those who favor either strategy. Stage
four highlights communication which heretofore has been the goal
of most methods, whether or not clearly stated or sufficiently emphasized. Explicitly stated or implicitly understood, oral communication is increasingly the goal of many learners of a second language,
particularly those going abroad. Stage five is especially significant
because it directs attention to the appropriateness of a communicative act. It recognizes that all speakers are judged as much for the
appropriateness of what they say as for how well they say it. It
requires that the learner acknowledge the social contextual factors
present at the moment of speech. In other words, the learner cannot
possibly speak appropriately unless he or she is also aware of
cultural factors which require the use of one linguistic form or
another.

For example, it is essential to learn verb endings which correspond to the various forms of "you" (such as *tu/vous* in French, *tu/
usted* in Spanish, *tu/lei/voi* in Italian). Knowledge of endings alone,
however, is not enough. The learner must also know when it is
appropriate to use each form, in what context, and with whom. This
requires information about the social system, the degree of familiarity or intimacy between speakers, and their status and roles. In other
words it is knowledge about the cultural system which underlies the
choice of one linguistic form or another. It is in this sense that
language and culture are clearly interrelated. Although most teachers profess to be concerned with the interrelationship of language
and culture, few utilize effective techniques for making this interrelationship explicit. Stage six looks specifically at the cultural context
of the target culture in which all communicative acts—as well as all
behavior—take place, since nothing happens in a vacuum, while
stage seven explores intercultural contrasts.

Although we have established several somewhat arbitrary stages in our process, these serve primarily as guideposts along a continuum. For convenience and clarity they are placed in sequential order. The sixth and seventh stages, however, when considered carefully, may be as much a part of the first stage as they are of the last. In fact, they transcend the entire process. Knowledge of culture and language go hand in hand, and the order of development is akin to the proverbial chicken and egg. Nevertheless the utility of this schema is: (1) to clarify objectives when choosing from among a variety of techniques, (2) to suggest a possible sequencing order of objectives and, therefore, techniques, (3) to permit the integration and use of all techniques regardless of the method from which derived, (4) to help evaluate methods in terms of how well they address the various aspects of language acquisition and language use, and (5) to direct attention to intercultural communicative competence which requires integration of both language and culture.

In the final analysis, the learner is required to be both linguist and ethnographer. One must learn not only the technology of a given language system, but the ways in which communication takes place in each context. One must acquire not only the ability to make linguistic constructs but also the cultural rules which govern their appropriateness. Because this is so, one is inevitably obliged to learn the total system of interactional strategies operative in a foreign setting, only part of which is language. The degree to which one is successful in both language and social interaction determines how rapidly and how effectively one functions abroad. In fact, such ability is the real passport for entry into a foreign culture.

References

Fantini, Alvino E. "The Promise of Intercultural Competence." In *Adult Learning* 2, no.5 (February 1991): 15-19.

Kelly, Louis G. *25 Centuries of Language Teaching*. Rowley, MA: Newbury House, 1969.

Mackey, William. "The Description of Bilingualism," by Joshua Fishman. In *Readings in the Sociology of Language*. The Hague: Mouton, 1970.

Martin, Judith N., guest ed. "Intercultural Communicative Competence" (Special Issue), *International Journal of Intercultural Relations* 13, no. 3 (1989).

Smith, Philip D. *A Comparison of the Cognitive and Audiolingual Approaches to Foreign Language Instruction*. Philadelphia: Center for Curriculum Development, 1970.

Part Two

ACTIVITIES

Introduction

Elizabeth Warner Christie

A long-held principle at The Experiment is the respect for exercises, games, or simulations as effective educational techniques, if chosen for specific purposes and conducted in a manner that helps the participants move toward the goals discussed by Anne Janeway in her introductory article.

On a practical level, we strongly urge you to experience an exercise yourself before deciding to use it with students or adult groups. And we even more strongly encourage you to consider why you are choosing a particular exercise, what it is intended to accomplish, and how it can contribute to your own broader teaching goals.

The exercises described here are a combination of strategies developed and used at The Experiment as well as those adapted from other sources. They range from specific techniques for language learning in the field to ways of teaching global sensitivity in the classroom. Although each exercise has its own purpose, they are all directed toward involving the learner as a whole person in the educational process.

Cross-cultural simulations—including The Owl, The Albatross, The Mockingbird, and The Ostrich—create opportunities for exploring the emotional and intellectual dynamics of preparing to enter another culture. Activities such as The Drop-Off and the Martian Anthropology exercise are offered as vehicles for developing observation skills by using the immediate environment in new and different ways. Other exercises offer a variety of ways to further enrich the cross-cultural learning experience.

6

Preparation for Cross-Cultural Experience

Donald Batchelder

There are many formulas for cross-cultural preparation. No single approach meets all of the needs of every student, group, institution, or academic director. A useful starting point, which has worked in the past, is to pose the following five questions and then conduct a series of exercises, activities, and discussions designed to engage the student with the issues they raise (noted in parentheses).

1. Who am I? (Self-awareness)
2. Where do I come from? (Awareness of U.S. culture, beliefs, values, etc.)
3. Where am I going? (Area information, the host culture, its expectations)
4. What for? (Purposes: learning, growth, language, interest in host country, self-motivation, others)
5. What am I willing to attempt? (Self-image, willingness, openness to participation, responsibility, effort, standards of performance, motivation, etc.)

Cross-cultural preparation has to be concerned with developing approaches to the overseas experience (1) which work for the individual and are suited to his or her personality, ways of seeing, ways of responding and reacting, and (2) which help the student to open up to communication, friendship, and learning in ways acceptable to the hosts. We try to take into account where individual students are, as learners and as people, recognizing that in any group there may be mixed motives, varied needs and expectations, and a sense of purpose that fluctuates from person to person and ranges from one end of the scale to the other. Without trying to impose an ideology, there are certain reasonable things we want for them.

- We want each participant to have as profound an experience abroad as his or her capacities allow.
- We want all students to reflect on the exceptional good fortune which enables them to have the support, resources, and opportunity for such an experience at this stage of their lives.
- We want them to open their receptors sufficiently to participate, to experience, to share in the daily life of the host country, and to enjoy both the culture and themselves in it.
- We want them to be interested observers and participants, as opposed to passive passengers with no questions to ask, no meanings to explore, and no interest in the cultural expressions around them.
- We want each student overseas to feel that he or she is lucky to be in that particular place, with those people, and to be able to say it, show it, and communicate it to the hosts.
- We want the host families, communities, and institutions to say at the end, "These are good young people. We are glad they came."
- We want each student to deal consciously with relationships and processes, as opposed to just dealing with factual data and content.
- We want each student to open up enough to try out new attitudes and behaviors in the development of appropriate responses to the new culture.
- We want each student to have the opportunity to develop in two important areas: self-awareness and cultural awareness.

Students tend to be comfortable intellectualizing about an up-coming overseas experience. While this is not totally useless, it can result in chronic intellectualizing overseas, as if one were still deal-ing with hypothetical situations and talking about people in remote locations rather than immersed in an actual situation filled with cross-cultural import, chances for real learning, and emotional im-pact. Further, students in orientation programs, unless challenged, often prefer to put off the start of the experience until they set foot on the soil of the host country.

Preparation should begin before the student leaves home or school. But the pressure of getting ready to depart, correspondence, packing, and other necessary things in addition to busy academic, social, and personal schedules leave scant time for deeper self-preparation. Students tend to arrive for predeparture orientation seldom having accomplished the basic reading one should do before reaching the host country. But at that stage the students are less in need of a map than a mechanism which will enable them to function well in the host culture. The available cultural orientation time (other than that which occurs within language class hours) is used to convey as much substance as possible through a process approach. Some staff presentations and lectures are employed, but generally the activities are designed to engage students in performance-based methodologies, roles, and simulations which deal with the five questions raised above and help develop human relations, observa-tion, and listening skills. Academic directors and cross-cultural trainers cannot force a student to engage in—or turn him or her on to—that critical process of becoming a cross-cultural sojourner. We can offer the apparatus and the current, but the student has to turn on the switch. Perhaps a brief sketch of some of the activities which center on the five questions will provide an adequate portrayal of the process.

Who Am I (Or, Who I Am)

Without getting into anything resembling sensitivity training, vari-ous group-dynamics exercises, including drama or role-play tech-niques, paired interviews, and others, bring out how students see themselves, how they are seen by others, what values they would not change, and what items they are willing to share with the group and want the group to know about. Here are some ideas:

1. A typical exercise asks each student to take a few minutes to write down what it is that makes his or her own family unique in the entire world. A good cross-cultural discussion can be generated on the basis of this. Rather than dealing with some abstraction or unknown town overseas, students become engaged in a deep discussion of something important and about which they are experts—their own families. Without much difficulty, the discussion can expand to deal with family and kinship in general, the host families overseas, the fact that all are special in some ways, etc.

2. Another useful device, almost a child's game, is to have each student write a color or an animal or the name of some natural object on a slip of paper. It should be chosen as somehow representative of the person writing it. The papers are then mixed and redistributed randomly, and the group goes through a weekend, a week, or the entire orientation period with members trying to figure out whose paper they are holding, the ground rule being that no direct questions can be asked. The intensity of listening and observing which takes place is remarkable and includes the added theatrics of suspense and mystery.

3. A useful way to begin orientation after basic introductions have been done is to use a simple device which serves two quick purposes: (a) it gets a lot of issues which are important to the participants out in the open early and (b) it tells the leader a great deal about where the group and some of its individual members are with regard to expectations, fears, motivation, etc. It usually becomes the basis for one of the first group discussions.

   To begin: have each group member take a sheet of paper and draw a line down the middle. In the left-hand column, ask them to list the three or four things they most anticipate, most look forward to, or feel especially good about in relation to the upcoming trip. In the right-hand column, ask them to list three or four things they are most concerned about, most worried about, most anxious, or most terrified of in relation to the experience. They are not asked to sign their names, so participants generally feel comfortable enough to state what is really on their minds.

Next, cut up the papers into anticipation and concerns, and put group members to work listing them on separate chalkboards or flip charts, using magic markers, in large enough script so everyone can see them. The items which are repeated can be combined with hash marks or asterisks indicating the number of mentions.

Next, have the group members who did the writing at the chalkboard read the items off one at a time, pausing long enough for a discussion of each one, being sure not to neglect those mentioned only once or twice. These latter items may be very important to the individual who listed them. It generally works best to read off and discuss the "looking forward to" set of responses first, which helps develop a sense of the overall expectations of the group and often provides some members with an opportunity to recognize a few of their own feelings and motivations which they had not yet articulated. Then move to the "concerned about" list and work through that as a group. If you find a lot of items centered on lost passports, getting sick, or being robbed, then you will know you have a lot of work to do in getting the group to begin to think about educational and cultural issues, but at the same time you will have a firm clue that you have people in the group who need considerable reassurance regarding personal safety and travel in general. Most often you will discover that you have a mixture of responses providing good discussion material which, again, is important because it comes from the group and from its immediate needs and priorities.

Where Do I Come From?

This question helps the students focus on American beliefs, values, behaviors, and viewpoints, how they came into being, and what they mean in a cross-cultural situation. The approaches to this question listed below have been used with considerable success.

1. One exercise is done in cooperation with the foreign students on our campus. Anywhere from 75 to 150 students complete short answers to such questions as:

   Americans are...

   Americans think that foreigners are...

   If an American had $5000 he or she would...

   American women are...

   American men are...

   With about 25 nationalities in the room, the answers are worth seeing and hearing, so they are written on great sheets of paper wrapped around the entire hall. While the answers are being compiled and attached to the walls, time can be spent in warm-up discussion, another brief exercise, or the showing of a short, provocative film such as *A Chairy Tale* (see Ellen Summerfield, *Crossing Cultures through Film*, Yarmouth, ME: Intercultural Press, 1993). The collected answers to each question are then read off in turn, and mixed American and foreign student groups participate in an all-campus intercultural workshop to thrash out some of the viewpoints expressed in answer to the questions. It is participatory, engaging, and provocative and requires careful listening and speaking as well as the sorting out of what is meant from what is actually said.

2. Another device which leaders have used with good results is that of asking the students to put themselves in the role of community chairperson of The Experiment program in their own home-towns in the United States. The task is to name ten host families in that hometown who can entertain students and visitors from the country to which the students are going. The students are then asked to describe their ten selected families and explain why each was chosen and what they have to offer the visitor. This is another device which engages the students in something with which they are familiar but have perhaps not thought about in these specific terms. What should the visitors see and experience? What does this family have to offer?

3. Try "Meet the Critic," alternatively called the Indian Interview or Americans on the Spot. A staff member plays the role of a critical

foreign observer and calls one or more students up front to sit at an improvised cafe table. He or she engages them in a discussion of such American phenomena as the breakdown of the family, slaughter on the highways, teen-age delinquency, the plight of minorities, materialism, change, progress, efficiency, manners, or any number of subjects based mainly on questions which host nationals and foreign visitors often raise about the U.S. and Americans. Foreign student advisors on college campuses can usually supply a good list of such questions.

4. Films and videos can be shown which highlight aspects of American life, such as homelessness, AIDS, crime, immigration (both historical and present), American trade practices, ecology, etc., followed by a discussion. Sometimes films and videos of this nature may be shown with foreign students in the audience. (See also Ellen Summerfield's book noted above.)

5. This is an exercise that helps group members relate where they are now to where they are coming from and where they want to go. It can be effective at various levels of transition (from their families in the U.S. to the homestay overseas), and in intellectual awareness and emotional and spiritual development. It taps a resource not used in many of the other exercises, that of visual imagery. You will need a box of crayons, enough paper for seven sheets per person, and a comfortable, quiet setting. You should tell your group that you are going to pose some questions to them and that you would like them to wait quietly for whatever image first comes into their minds and then draw it on a piece of paper. It may be an abstract design, a color, a clear representation, a form—it doesn't matter. It is a good idea to have them close their eyes and take three or five deep breaths before each question, to allow them to be more open to images. When you have finished with the seven questions, invite them to share their drawings with each other—perhaps in smaller groups of two or three. If someone doesn't want to share, don't press him or her—but invite that person to join one of the groups anyway. Be sure to try this exercise with other leaders or with friends before you try it with your group so you can get a feel for the process. These are the questions:

1. Where am I now?
2. Where am I coming from?
3. What does change mean to me?
4. What would I like my life to be?
5. What do I need to get there?
6. What's stopping me?
7. What self-portrait do I draw of myself?

This exercise is useful in getting group members to look at themselves honestly at this time in their lives and in getting them to open up to one another and develop feelings of trust and respect within the group by sharing experience and communicating feelings verbally and nonverbally.

Where Am I Going?

A great deal of host-country realia is introduced in the language classrooms and orientation activities emphasizing manners, family roles, and lifestyles. Role plays, scenarios involving the use of language and videos, and slide presentations in the language are employed. Host-country songs are learned, and groups plan and prepare a typical host-country dinner at a staff home, etc. Academic directors and staff make substantive area-studies presentations as needed, and considerable time is devoted to sampling and discussing the way of life of the host country and ways in which American views and behaviors may need to be modified in order to achieve acceptance on host-country terms.

1. What are the values, beliefs, and ways which make sense to the host nationals; how did they come about; and what is their meaning for us as Americans? Answering these questions calls for the development of suitable approaches to the host culture and its people, respect for their ways, accepting the idea of the American student as the stranger and the outsider, empathizing with the sense of place of the host nationals (the importance of their town and their country to them, it being the center of the world as far as they are concerned). Cultural simulations and related activities are employed to engage the students fully. Case studies from previous programs are examined and frequently acted out and discussed.

2. As in number 2 of "Where Do I Come From," have the leader get each member of the group to play the role of The Experiment representative from his or her own hometown in the United States. Each representative is responsible for finding 10 or 12 homestays for a group of foreigners.

   Procedure: Give each new participant a piece of paper and have each one write down the names of 10 or 12 families which would be ideal or good host families. Problem: Finding 10 or 12 "typical" American families. Questions:

   (a) In each town, would all of the families expect and accept the same kind of behavior?

   (b) Can we generalize about the attitudes these families might have regarding religion, politics, dating, etc.?

   (c) What sort of attitudes should the Experimenter from another country have if he or she is to be successful in a homestay with these families? This is done because a lot of time would otherwise be wasted in getting people to project themselves into the total unknown of a host community or family overseas, and because discussion would have to be carried on very abstractly at times. This device enables them to talk about gut issues in a setting with which they are very familiar—their own hometowns.

3. Have each person draw, freehand and from memory, the country he or she is to be visiting. Ask them to try to include everything they know or can remember and allow them to make some guesses. Have the group compile their individual maps into one map, either on a large sheet of paper or a blackboard. Introduce a commercial map. Compare and discuss. This can lead to questions and inferences of why sites are located where they are, i.e., cities in relation to bodies of water; major transport routes in relation to mountains, coasts, etc.; climate and population concentration; resources and settlement; the location of industry. This type of exercise helps familiarize people with the geographic information of an area and also gives meaning and reason to particular facts such as city locations, boundaries, resort areas, employment, and other features of human geography. It increases peoples' ability to observe and stimulates questions that can be asked about any place visited.

What For?

Expectations, both on the part of the student and the host nationals, are considered. Role plays and case studies are employed, and staff engage the students in individual and group discussions of their goals, both academic and personal. For example, in study abroad programs we find it helpful to stage a discussion in which the students describe their study projects for the overseas term. It quickly becomes apparent that some students have very clearly defined, well-planned study programs, while others are unclear or uncertain about the courses they plan to take or study projects they have outlined. This process leads to a general upgrading of the study project through shared discussion and to clarification for those who need it. A sequel to this discussion is the process of sorting out the balance between specific study objectives and the overall field experience in the host country. We are committed to the idea of developing cross-cultural learning skills and try to provide the students with experiences in orientation that build skills which they can transfer overseas to make them better participants, observers, and cross-cultural sojourners. We start with a basic belief that each student has his or her own special qualities either well in hand or in the process of development and that the potential for dynamic growth in self-awareness and cultural awareness is within reach of each student who takes the trouble to grasp it. Individual and group goals are discussed early in the process and, as the orientation program progresses, two elements of the goal-setting process are emphasized: (a) realistic expectations and (b) a gradual increase in willingness to make the effort to learn the needed skills. We attempt to help students see the ways in which this intercultural experience relates to the rest of their lives—past, present, and future.

What Am I Willing to Attempt?

This is a catchall category related directly to the preceding one. It focuses on a willingness to make the effort, to set some high standards for learning, participating, getting along, and seeing other viewpoints. We employ a variety of engagement processes, as illustrated by exercises in this volume:

1. The Albatross exercise, in which students are admitted to a mythical culture where all cues and communications are carried out nonverbally and where assumptions about the ways to react differ markedly from those based on American models.

2. The Martian Anthropology exercise, where students are placed in the role of anthropologists from another planet and are sent to American institutions such as Laundromats (to observe American science in action), to supermarkets (to study agriculture and crop production), to banks (to study religious rituals), to the bus station (to study American family life), to a pub (to observe family and kinship), etc.

3. The Drop-Off exercise, a community investigation technique based on anthropological and sociological models, which students can practice in local towns during orientation and then use in the overseas host community as a framework for more specific study and observation.

These examples may help to identify the approaches employed, but the limits of space prohibit a detailed rendering of precise schedules and sequences or the ways in which one exercise or activity follows another. It is probably clear, however, that most of these require active engagement on the part of the students.

By the time students leave the orientation program, most of them have worked things through in their own minds, individually and collectively, to a point where they are willing to give the cross-cultural experience a good try. They are generally quite confident that they can adapt successfully, and some are quite certain that we have made a big fuss over cross-cultural issues which they knew about all along. It is normal for them to credit themselves, rather than us, for any new insights, understanding, or clarifications they may have gained, and we can live with that.

We emphasize the concepts of learning how to learn through experience, including how to study, observe, record, and categorize. We emphasize strongly the management of personal relationships with one another and with the people they meet overseas. While doing this, we recognize that the passage of time is an important element in the process. We have to let things happen, unfold, or open up over the orientation period, as anticipation builds toward departure.

The same time element is at work overseas. Experimenters may not be as ready or as fully prepared as we would like them to be at departure time, but they are generally better prepared than would be the case with no orientation at all. Change and movement take place overseas as they progress through successive experiences, conflicts, resolutions, confrontations, and epiphanies. These latter are what some teachers refer to as "learning moments."

The academic director or leader with the group overseas carries on an ongoing orientation and training process while the students are experiencing the host culture. The growth of self-awareness and cultural awareness is observed carefully by both leaders and students, with the recognition that assessment at regular intervals is essential to tracking the growth and learning that take place. The following categories serve as guidelines for assessment and springboards for identifying additional areas of growth:

1. Self-awareness, inner growth, maturity
   Willingness to accept responsibility for oneself, one's actions, and one's impact on the external world. Growth in autonomy, inner-directedness, self-reliance. Development of perspective, balance, judgment. Interest in people, in host culture, in things outside the individual. Evidence of participation, involvement.

2. Learning how to learn
   Interest in learning, openness to new experiences. Development of insight into one's own learning processes. Setting of realistic learning objectives and choice of means. Skill in planning and setting priorities, initiative, discipline. Evidence of reflection on one's experiences.

3. Adaptability and adjustment
   Evidence of interest in program and commitment to it. Receptivity to new ways, new ideas, new people. Emotional steadiness or balance. Ability to handle ambiguity. Ability to see a broader context than the isolated experience. Physical stamina, recovery capability, resiliency.

4. Knowledge and awareness of host culture
   Factual information. Understanding of complexity and interrelatedness or patterns. Awareness of implications of one's own

acts and their impact on external events. Insight into the meaning of things in the culture, its symbols, and how the culture works. Sensitivity to values, artistic and cultural achievements.

5. Skill in action or effectiveness
   Assessment of situations and appropriateness of response. Development of needed tools of communication. Development of powers of observation and analysis and the ability to give and receive feedback. Motivation and ability to apply knowledge and insight gained. Awareness of cultural relativity, of oneself as a cultural being. Appreciation of the host culture and of the values of international understanding.

7

A Short Guide to Designing and Conducting an Experiential Exercise

Claude Pepin

As a teacher or trainer interested in using an experiential exercise, you have three options available: (1) design a new one, (2) adapt an existing exercise to fit your purposes, or (3) employ one which seems well suited to your particular situation. In any of the three cases, the following questions and steps can serve as guidelines in preparing the exercise.

Observation Exercise: Student Group to Ghana

I. Consider the participants

Questions	Facts and Assumptions
• Who and how many are they?	Twenty U.S. college students going to Ghana for three months.
• What are their backgrounds/ experiences?	Two have visited Europe and Mexico. Thirteen have limited travel experience. All come from traditional university settings. None speaks Twi. Urban and sub-

Questions	Facts and Assumptions
	urban middle, upper-middle class. Five black, fifteen white. Major study fields varied.
• What are their expectations?	Lecture or seminar on observation skills. Presentation of specific information about Ghana. Not expecting to see each other or themselves as resources for learning observation skills.
• In what ways can their skills, energies, and needs be utilized?	Make use of their enthusiasm as an energizing force. Use the fact that two have been to West Africa; use the fact that they have a wealth of observation experience among them, perhaps not consciously employed; use their hunger for culture-specific information about Ghana.

II. Clearly define your purposes

If an exercise is to be an effective learning experience, it must be designed to bring about full participation by the learners and must have its objectives—what is to be learned—clearly defined.

Questions	Facts and Assumptions
• Given the participants, their expectations and needs, what do you expect them to learn?	To understand that observations, judgments, and actions may be based totally upon past experiences in their own culture.
• What are the key issues or significant points to be examined?	The difference between observation and judgment; relationship of personal experience to what one does/does not see/ does value; the fact that there is no single definition of any culture or nation-state, that one's own set of observations, perceptions, and judgments comprises a continually changing definition of reality on which one acts each day (there are many

Questions	Facts and Assumptions
	ways to observe: seeing, listening, feeling, sensing, smelling, tasting, intuition); the importance of suspending final judgment by means of formulating low-level hypotheses which can be upgraded with new experience and observation; the fact that improved skills in observation, perception, and judgment will enhance one's effectiveness and enjoyment in another culture.

Note: The purpose of the exercise should be clearly defined. If a participant experiences it fully, what will she or he learn? In addition to the overall purpose, there are also subpurposes or "learning points" along the way. For example, in this case the purpose is to focus on the influences of past experience upon observation, judgment, and subsequent action. A representative learning point which leads up to that purpose could be defined as learning how past experience influences observation, judgment, and perception in new situations and in different cultural contexts. Another learning point might be an examination of these elements as preludes to appropriate or inappropriate action in the American context or the Ghanian context.

III. Ways and means

Questions	Facts And Assumptions
• What are alternative ways to accomplish this purpose and these learning points?	Discussions of selected readings. Role play of a typical Ghanian scene. A series of slides about Ghanian life. A short film about Ghana. Lecture by a Ghanian guest. An activity which requires participants to observe and to take action.
• How did I learn these things in my own life?	Common experience of sharing an episode or event with someone else and reaching two different conclusions.

Questions	Facts And Assumptions
	The first time I was treated by a female physician.
	My first exposure to sharp criticism of U.S. foreign policy by someone from another culture.

At this stage it might be more useful and productive to generate imaginative ideas to meet your purpose, rather than thinking of constraints and trying to design the exercise around them. Constraints can be applied too quickly to the seed of a creative idea. Try to keep in mind the learning points you have identified. The exercise you choose should ideally allow each participant the opportunity to relate to the experience in his or her individual way.

The following questions will guide you in considering the relative merits of various exercises you might want to use:

1. How much time will I have to conduct the exercise or activity and the discussion?
2. How much time do I have to prepare?
3. What resources do I have available (space, people, materials, etc.)?
4. What assumptions have I made about the participants, the materials, and other factors?
5. What questions will be useful and appropriate for discussion?

Some questions appropriate for an observation exercise might be:

- What did you observe?
- Are you talking about observations or judgments?
- Did other people observe the same things you did? Why or why not?
- How did your assumptions influence what you observed?
- What do you need to learn to free your observations from your personal biases or the limitations of your personal experience or knowledge?

One of the most important parts of any exercise is the discussion afterwards. In the case of experiential activities there is a sequence which usually makes sense.

After a shared experience, the first question to the group needs to be one which draws out the nature of the experience. It in some way asks. What happened? What did others do? What did you see? The intention here is to create a common description.

In most cases you will want to follow this by going to a second level in which participants are asked to describe their reactions to the experience, especially talking about the emotions they felt in highly charged activities and situations. This allows for the expression of immediate responses and serves to express and diffuse excitement, confusion, or adverse reactions to the activity itself. Here it is important that the facilitator accept the statements made as valid information and grist for further discussion.

Next come "why" questions, which draw out the assumptions the participants brought to the experience and what they inferred from it, such questions as: Why did you think that? Why did you feel that? Why do you think they did that?

Normally, only after this processing of the immediate experience, the participants' reactions, and their inferences is it possible to move the discussion to abstractions. Here questions need to forge the link between the experience and larger concepts and principles. What have you learned about yourself as an observer? What in this exercise might be parallel to other cross-cultural experiences? Which of the conclusions we have drawn here might work in Ghana (or another culture)? Which might not?

Finally, have the participants evaluate the exercise as a whole to assess whether or not its original purpose has been achieved.

8

Language and Intercultural Orientation: A Process Approach

Alvino E. Fantini and William P. Dant

The goal of most language and intercultural orientation programs is to prepare individuals to function effectively in a foreign culture. To accomplish this, programs commonly contain various components, including language study, intercultural orientation, and area studies. The purpose is to prepare the total individual. The language teacher, as a member of the orientation staff, has an important role in this preparation.

The main objective of the language component is to develop competence in the communication strategies appropriate to the host culture. The emphasis is on oral skills and interactional strategies. A core text may be available with suggested exercises, supplemented by visual aids, tape recordings, and handouts with additional techniques. No matter what materials are selected or developed by the teacher, however, the focus remains on the development of language acquisition, which suggests, in turn, stages in the teaching process.

These seven stages are discussed in detail by Fantini in another article in this volume ("Focus on Process: An Examination of the

Learning and Teaching of Intercultural Communicative Competence"). Although somewhat arbitrarily constituted, these stages provide a useful framework for attending to various dimensions of language acquisition and suggest the structure for the "Sample Lesson and Schema" which appears below.

Although not meant to be limiting, a process approach helps to guide both teacher and learner through various aspects of the language-development process. It aids the teacher by helping to clarify objectives of each learning activity selected and by suggesting possible sequencing. Its intent is to encourage synthesis of all that is known about teaching and learning. Its approach is optimum matching of the student, the teacher, the context, and the process. One hopes that its results are intercultural communicative competence appropriate to the host culture.

The sections that follow illustrate how the process approach can be translated into specific lessons, with special emphasis on transposition techniques (stage four) and sociolinguistic exploration (stage five), since language teachers are generally already familiar with techniques which address stages one through three. Although the sections relating to stages four and five are divided into ten sections corresponding to the ten units of a specific language text, they may be used in any order and adapted for use with any other materials. Techniques which fit stages six and seven may be found in a variety of intercultural training materials, as well as in *Cross-Cultural Orientation: A Guide for Leaders and Educators* (The Experiment in International Living, Brattleboro, Vermont, 1984).

Process Approach to Teaching/Learning
A Sample Lesson and Schema:

Stage	Possible Techniques
1. Presentation of new material	1. A full or abbreviated dialogue
	2. A two-line exchange (Q & A)
	3. Colored rods
	4. _____
	5. _____

Stage	Possible Techniques
2. Practice in context	1. Repetition drills
	2. Pattern practice (all types of drills)
	3. Controlled narrative and questions
	4. _____
	5. _____
3. Explanation	1. Grammatical explanation
	2. _____
	3. _____
4. Transposition	1. Structured or unstructured conversation
	2. Games
	3. Free narratives/role plays
	4. Visual aids/flannelboards, etc.
	5. _____
5. Sociolinguistic exploration	1. Listening to native speakers for specific linguistic items
	2. Questioning native speakers
	3. Observation of native speakers in real settings
	4. _____
	5. _____
6. Cultural exploration	1. _____
	2. _____
	3. _____
7. Intercultural exploration	1. _____
	2. _____
	3. _____

Transposition Techniques

The following exercises and activities focus on communication tasks. They differ from activities of the previous steps primarily in that their main concern is with the message rather than the form of speech. These suggestions are designed to serve as starters. Teachers are encouraged to develop other similar activities as appropriate to their needs.

UNIT I: Before the Trip

1. Have the students tell where they are planning to stay in the country they are going to and say something factual about it.
2. Bring into class a bag of objects related to different destinations: maps of towns and countries, transportation tickets, guidebooks, a passport, a bathing suit, etc. Have each student draw an object from the bag which represents his or her destination. Another student then asks where the person with the object is going and the person replies.
3. Find a photo or picture of people which suggests travel. Have students assume the identities of the people in the picture. Be sure to choose a picture which will allow them to use words and structures which they have learned. Or simply ask them to describe the picture.
4. Have each student talk for one minute without interruption about his or her travel plans.
5. Have students converse (in the language they are studying) with someone who can speak it other than yourself. Ask them to talk about their travel plans and to try to make a good impression on the person with whom they talk. Have them report back to the class later on the conversation.
6. Ask two students to imagine that they are meeting in the street. Have one tell the other about where he or she is going.

UNIT II: En route

1. Suggest to the class some emotional situations in which they might find themselves: being late for class, being in an accident, finding $100, receiving a letter conveying bad news, etc. Ask the students to describe how they would feel in a given situation

and, if possible, why.

2. Have students ask and answer questions concerning their own and each others' roles and identities.

3. Have students give a lecture on the geography of a country which they expect to visit or on their hometown or country. Encourage them to use a map and any other supportive material available (pictures, postcards, posters, slides, etc.).

4. Have each student talk for one minute without interruption about his or her daily activities.

5. Set up a situation between pairs of students where one student plays him- or herself and the other plays the role of a fellow plane/train/bus/boat passenger. Have them strike up a conversation. Help the students if they ask for a word or expression, but do not interrupt to correct them. Take discreet notes on their mistakes, which you can talk about afterwards if you think it useful.

6. As in number 5 in Unit I ("Before the Trip"), have the students find someone who speaks the language other than yourself and discuss with that person the program he or she is enrolled in. Then have the students report back to the class.

7. GAME: *Going on a Trip.* One student, or the teacher, begins the game by saying, "I'm going on a trip and I'm putting _____ in my suitcase" (something which the students are capable of saying). The next person repeats what the teacher or first student has said, adding a second item. The next person repeats the sentence, adding a third item, and so on. A student is excluded from the game when he or she cannot remember all the items previously said.

8. Make up an exercise revolving around preparations for a trip (shopping, making reservations, buying tickets, getting a passport, going to the airport/station, checking in, etc.). You may introduce new vocabulary, but try to build the exercise around vocabulary which students already know, and use only verb tenses and grammatical structures already taught.

9. Set up a situation in which one person is asking another one for personal information: name, address, birthday, marital status, profession, etc. Keep the situation simple enough for your students to handle, but try to keep the questions asked as similar as

possible to real questions they will probably hear abroad. In order to model the questions, you may want to play the role of the person asking (an immigration officer, a policeman, or another official). Then let the students play both roles.

10. Have each student talk without interruption for one minute about the things he or she will take on a trip.

11. As in the previous units, have them converse with someone who speaks the language other than yourself, asking the students to talk about their own families or the families with whom they may be living while abroad.

UNIT III: Meeting the Family

1. Think of a series of situations in which the students might be called on to make introductions or be introduced. Write each situation on a small card and give one to each student. They in turn read the situation aloud and choose others in the class to act it out. Help them if they need it, but try not to interrupt for corrections.

2. GAME: *Colors and Rhythm.* Each member of the class chooses a color which is his or hers for the game. The group is seated in a circle and begins a rhythmic clapping: two claps on the knees, followed by two claps of the hands. The game begins with the first handclap, at which time one person says his or her own color and, on the second handclap, the color of another player. The player called must do the same, i.e., say his or her own color on the next handclap and another player's color on the following. When a player makes a mistake, misses a clap, or can't think of a color in time for the clap, then he or she is eliminated and the person who came just before continues the game. The winner is the last person left. This exercise can be done with words in categories other than color.

3. Draw your family tree on the blackboard, explaining basic family relationships only as far as the students' knowledge of the language will permit. Then have students come to the board and do the same. Have other students ask details about the families, using basic question patterns learned so far (who? where? what? why? etc.).

4. GAME: *This is my* ___ . The teacher begins by going to a student and saying a complete sentence, for example, "This is my mouth," while pointing to his or her hand and beginning to count to ten. Before ten is reached, the student must point to his or her mouth and say, "This is my hand." The student who fails to do so or makes a mistake is then "it" and must do the same thing to other students until someone else makes a mistake. The game ends when everybody becomes hysterical or bored.
5. Bring in a picture showing something about a family from a country where the language of study is spoken.
6. Have each student talk for one minute fluently (or two minutes less fluently) about his or her family, using personal pictures if possible.
7. As in the previous units, have them converse with someone who speaks the language other than yourself, asking the students to compare their families with the other person's family.

UNIT IV: At the Host Family's Home
1. Find or draw a plan which shows a typical house with furniture usually found in a country where the target language is spoken, labeling parts of the plan in that language. Distribute copies of the house plan or draw it on the board while discussing it.
2. Describe the layout of your own house to the students and ask them to draw the house plan as you talk. Then draw your house plan on the board and compare the different versions.
3. Ask the students to draw simple layouts of their homes and have each exchange the layout with another student. Then have each describe the other's plan.
4. Prepare and distribute copies of a train, bus, and/or plane schedule to each student. Have students work on the structures and vocabulary that they have learned related to time, distances, travel times, etc.
5. Have each student talk for one minute fluently (or two minutes less fluently) about the clothing he or she is wearing.
6. As in previous units, have them converse with someone who speaks the language other than yourself, asking the students to talk about transportation in the country where they are going.

UNIT V: At the Table
1. Find or make a restaurant menu used in a country where the target language is spoken. Distribute a copy to each student. First explain any terms with which the students are unfamiliar. Then have students work on the structures and vocabulary they have learned so far
2. Create situations which will allow the students to act in a simulated environment related to eating:
   (a) as a guest for a meal at someone's home,
   (b) as a member of a family abroad at mealtime,
   (c) in a restaurant abroad.

If the students are beginners, you may prefer to model a situation first, using a short dialogue containing mostly familiar material. This will provide them with some of the vocabulary and structures necessary for the situation. If the students are more confident in their abilities, you may give them the situations and have them prepare for a few minutes on their own, or even react immediately if they seem ready. Once the students begin, let them act out the situation without interruption.

3. Ask each student to write down his or her favorite meal. The teacher should do the same on the board. The students may not know how to say everything, so help them while they are writing their own menus. Then have students question each other about their food likes and dislikes.
4. Have each student speak for one minute fluently (or two minutes less fluently) about what he or she usually eats for breakfast, lunch, or dinner.
5. As in previous units, have the students converse with someone who speaks the language other than yourself, this time about eating customs in the U.S. and abroad.

UNIT VI: A Visit to the City
1. Find or make a city map from a country where the target language is spoken. Try to use one which shows monuments or shops clearly. Make a copy for each student. Make up cards saying, for example, "You are at ___ and want to go to ____. Ask for directions." Be sure students know how to ask for and give the directions required by the cards. Teach any necessary

expressions and vocabulary they don't know by modeling the expected responses in one or two of the cards and having the students repeat. The student drawing the card must then go to another member of the class and ask for directions. The person asked must give directions according to the map handed out.

2. Make up a list of typical addresses and telephone numbers as they exist in a country where the target language is spoken. Give a copy to each student and have him or her practice reading it. Also have the students give their own home addresses in the target language. Finally, dictate some other addresses and phone numbers to help them understand this sort of information more easily.

   N.B.: Be sure your class has learned basic numbers and the alphabet before attempting this exercise.

3. Use the same city map as in exercise 1, or find another map which clearly shows physical details (hills, rivers, parks, bridges, monuments, buildings) and distribute it to the class. Have students work on structures and vocabulary related to the different aspects of your map.

4. Have each student research a famous monument in a country where the target language is spoken and prepare a short talk, using visual aids available (pictures, posters, slides, etc.). Urge students to keep their talk within their linguistic capabilities.

5. Have each student converse with someone other than yourself who speaks the target language and who is familiar with a country where this language is spoken. Have the student find out, in the language of study, as much as possible about some geographical feature of the country (rivers, mountains, cities, oceans, agriculture, industry, population, demography), and report back to the class.

6. Have each student speak fluently for one minute (or two minutes less fluently) about the geographical features of his or her home region or state.

UNIT VII: At a Cafe/Restaurant/Bar

1. Set up a cafe or bar situation in the classroom. Have students play the roles of friends meeting there, ordering refreshments, talking, etc. The teacher can play the waiter in order to give a

realistic representation of what the students can expect to hear in a similar situation abroad. Or if students are more confident, the teacher can choose a student to play the role of the waiter.

2. Assign each student a type of shop or place of business in a country where the language of study is spoken. Have them research the functions, hours, etc. of the shop and prepare a short report for the class.

3. Have students use new vocabulary they have learned by assigning them roles of different merchants or tradesmen they have learned about so far in the class.

4. If possible, bring into class some real money from a country where the target language is spoken. Go over vocabulary particular to the currency (common names of coins, like "nickel," "dime," etc.) as well as any simple, necessary expressions which normally accompany the use of money ("Do you have change?", "How much does it cost?", etc.); then have students practice asking for and making change, inquiring about prices, etc.

5. As in previous units, have the students converse with a person who speaks the language other than yourself, asking them to find out about money in some other country where the language is spoken or more about the currency and its use in the country already studied.

6. Set up a bank or currency exchange role play.

UNIT VIII: A Shopping Trip

1. Have each student make up a list of gifts or things he or she wants to buy abroad and then describe the list to the class indicating where it will most likely be possible to purchase each item.

2. Find a picture showing a shopping or market scene and develop an exercise using the grammar and vocabulary students have learned up to this point.

3. GAME: *I'm going to* _____ *and I'm going to buy* _____ . The teacher begins the game by saying, "I'm going to (the name of a shop or place of business) and I'm going to buy (something which can be bought there)." The teacher then gives the name of another shop and asks a student to make a similar sentence. The

game continues with each student. When a student cannot think (in the language of study) of an item to buy, or names an inappropriate object (within the culture of the language studied), or gives a name which has already been said by another person, he or she is eliminated from the game.

4. Set up a shop situation in which a student must buy an item from a shopkeeper, played by another student or the teacher. Write down, one to a card, a number of tasks such as, "You want to buy a roll of film" or "You need a bottle of aspirin," and have each student draw a card and respond to it. The teacher can either introduce the shopkeeper's phrases needed or begin by playing the shopkeeper's role before asking other students to do so.

5. As in previous units, have the students converse with a person who speaks the language other than yourself, asking them to find out about articles of food which are typical of a country or region of a country where the target language is spoken.

UNIT IX: At the Post Office

1. Go through the steps of letter writing (e.g., "I take a piece of paper and a pen. I write the date. I write the letter. I sign it. I fold the letter. I take an envelope," etc.). Or, if the language uses reflexive verbs, create an operation around those verbs.

2. Set up a post office situation and give the students cards telling them what they must do. ("Have this letter weighed and buy stamps for it," "Send a telegram, mail a postcard, make a phone call to the U.S.," etc.). You or a capable student can play the role of the postal clerk.

3. Have your students practice writing a simple letter. Be sure to give them the basic format for letter writing in the target language (where and how to write the date, salutation, body of the letter, the end and signature). Then have them read their letters aloud to the class, helping as called for. A good practice letter would be a thank-you note to a family who has invited the student into their home.

4. Ask each student about the most recent letter he or she has received—where it came from, who wrote it, and that person's relationship to the student.

Sociolinguistic Exploration

Mastery of a language involves not only the ability to use structure and vocabulary with grammatical correctness, but also appropriately: the right thing said in the right manner at the right time to the right person. This requires use of appropriate paralanguage (pitch, speed, volume, tone, and other affective qualities of the voice) as well as extralinguistic or nonverbal aspects of the communication system (gestures, the appropriate use of time and space, touch and eye-contact patterns, etc.). For this reason, students need to explore sociolinguistic dimensions appropriate to the host culture. The following tasks are designed with that in mind.

UNIT I: Before the Trip

1. Find out how to greet and say good-bye properly to the variety of people you are likely to meet or come into contact with during the first week of a stay abroad. With your teacher's or another person's help, you should be able to get this information through a trial-and-error process.
2. Make a list of the kinds of people you think you would generally address with one or another form of the second-person pronoun, if more than one form exists. Consult your teacher or another person knowledgeable in the target language to verify your list, and try to find out why each person would be addressed in one or another way.
3. Observe your teacher's gestures or facial expressions when he or she is speaking the target language. Are there differences between these "signals" and those which you might make when speaking English? Concentrate on one gesture or expression and try to find out when it is appropriate and what it means. Are these gestures appropriate only to male speakers? Female speakers? Both?
4. Explore ways of expressing gratitude in the host culture. Are there variations of "thank you"? When are they appropriate?

UNIT II: En route

1. Find out the equivalent of your name and the names of others in your class, if they exist in the target language. Find out if there

are any diminutives which can be used with these names; if so, when are they used? What special meaning does the diminutive connote?

2. Find out what speakers of the target language are generally called by people who have different relationships with them. Find out what degree of intimacy is necessary before you can pass from a more formal to a more familiar form of address.
3. Find out how you would address those people you might meet in the first week of your stay abroad and whether the place you might meet them would affect your behavior.
4. Explore how individuals of the host culture use space, that is, how close do they stand to each other? Do they stand in line (queue up)? At what points does distance convey intimate, casual, or formal relationships?
5. What kind of eye contact is appropriate? Is the same eye contact used with males and females? Children? Older people?
6. Find out what to expect in the country you might visit as far as dealing with persons in an official capacity (customs officers, immigration agents, policemen, etc.). Are there special titles of address, forms of speech, bribes/tips which are appropriate or expected in certain situations?
7. In the U.S., we divide the day into A.M. and P.M. How does the host culture distinguish between morning and afternoon time? Are there various ways of telling time? How is time usually posted on official schedules?
8. Time and its efficient use are important to many Americans. We think of Americans as generally prompt and serious about appointment times. Find out what the general attitude toward time, punctuality, and waiting is in the target culture. What expressions in the language reflect these attitudes?

UNIT III: Meeting the Family

1. Find out from an informant what the word "family" signifies in his or her culture. Find out the same information for the word "friend." Are there special words to designate people who are other than friends or family with whom one has a relationship?
2. When seeing someone, whether it be for the first time or not, there is generally more than just a verbal side to greeting and

leave-taking. Review your list of people to greet and say good-
bye to, and find out what physical manifestations (handshakes,
bows, embracing, kissing) are most appropriate for each person
and in what circumstances.

3. Find out *why* people physically greet and take leave of each other
as they do. What might make you change the degree of intimacy
with which you approach or touch them? How would an inappropriate greeting or farewell be interpreted?

4. Find out what the usual reactions are to different kinds of
compliments in the language you are studying. What should
you say when someone compliments you on the way you speak
the target language? On something you have which they like?

UNIT IV: At the Host Family's Home

1. Most languages have an expression similar to the English "make
yourself at home." Investigate the meaning of this expression
within the culture of the country you will be visiting. Also, what
are the connotations of the word "guest"?

2. What are the topographical boundaries and limitations of a
"home" in the country to which you are going? What status does
"your" room have for others in the family? What status do the
other rooms have for you and other family members? Private?
Public? Knock before entering? How important are doors in
defining public and private space? Are doors to be kept open or
closed?

3. As natural or universal as they may seem, daily "bathroom"
matters are viewed and dealt with differently from culture to
culture. They are therefore often hard to talk about properly in
a foreign language. Find out from an informant what is said
relating to your trips to the bathroom and to any other etiquette
related to it. Find out what the word "bathroom" means. What
can you expect to find in it: tub, shower, bidet, toilet?

4. How loud is it customary to speak in the home? In a public
place? What is the direction of conversation? Do several persons
speak at the same time, or does only one person talk at a time?

UNIT V: At the Table

1. Find out the appropriate ways in which you can express your needs at the table. What should you do, for example, if you want more, or if you are full? How do you politely refuse? How many times do people normally offer guests the servings? What rituals might you have to follow to leave the table? Should you leave before anyone else does?

2. Continue your investigation of the meaning of "make yourself at home" and "guest" as related to eating and meals. What are the responsibilities of someone who is "making herself (himself) at home" and someone who is a "guest"? What should one normally offer to do, and to what extent are refusals or acceptances of services offered to be taken literally?

3. Most cultures have prescribed habits concerning hands and eating. Differences can vary from the ways a knife and fork are held or where the bread is placed, to taboos concerning the right or left hand and where it may be placed. Find out which habits or customs are different but do not necessarily need to be adhered to, which customs do need to be adhered to, and which of your customs are taboo or offensive to people in the country you are visiting.

4. What do people usually say to one another the first thing in the morning and before going to bed at night?

UNIT VI: A Visit to the City

1. Do you know how to express distances, weights, measurements, temperature in the system of the country you will be visiting?

2. Whom do you ask for information on a public street? Can you approach a person of either sex? Of any age? Or should you seek out an officer? In what other places can you obtain information about a town you may be visiting and what it offers of interest?

3. How do you hail a bus? A taxi? Do you need small change? What is considered an unreasonably high charge? Do you tip? What do you say during these transactions?

4. Investigate the meaning of the word "old" in the target language. How old are buildings which are called "old"? What are the attitudes of people in the country you will visit regarding old

things? And what feelings do the words "new" and "modern" conjure up in the minds of your hosts?

5. Similarly, what is an old person? Find out when a person is considered old and what attitude people from the culture have toward this person. What role and status do young people have? Is age discussed at all? Is it appropriate to ask someone's age?

6. To an American, mention of the White House, the Golden Gate Bridge, or the Statue of Liberty conjure up more thoughts than just the image of a house, a bridge, or a statue. Find out which well-known places in the host country trigger similar reactions in the people who live there. While investigating, try to deepen your knowledge of the history and traditions of the country.

UNIT VII: At a Cafe/Restaurant/Bar

1. Investigate the range of products and services offered by different shops in the host country. Make a list of the goods or services which interest you and find out where one would go for them.

2. Sometimes Americans have the reputation of being careless with their expenses, wasteful or, on the other hand, tight or cheap. These impressions may be based on Americans reacting differently in certain social situations. Find out when you should offer to share the cost of something or pay for a friend or, conversely, when you should accept such offers from others. Investigate the possibilities of offending someone because of different customs concerning picking up a tab, tipping, having a drink with someone, etc. Find out what is normally said and done on these occasions.

3. How would you ask a person of the opposite sex to go out with you (possibly on a date, if permissible)? Would you ask the person or his or her parents? Under what conditions would you accept a similar invitation? What is said?

4. What are the words for "boyfriend" and "girlfriend," and what do they mean in comparison with the American definition? What other terms are used and what are their connotations?

5. What are the ways of calling a waiter or waitress in the host country? Are there certain procedures for ordering and asking for the bill? Is there normally a service charge, cover charge, or tax added to the bill?

UNIT VIII: A Shopping Trip

1. How do you approach various people for help, information, etc.? How do you gain the attention of a shopkeeper? Salesperson? How do you fend off aggressive vendors, especially in the streets? What kinds of things should you say?
2. If you bump into a person or step on someone's toes, how do you excuse yourself? What kinds of things are appropriate to say?
3. In many countries bargaining over prices is accepted and expected by merchants. If such is the case in the country you will visit, ask an informant to help you with bargaining techniques and find out the necessary expressions for these transactions.
4. Find out the importance of gift giving in the host culture. When is a gift appropriate, and what is appropriate in the situation? When is a gift necessary, and when is one not expected? How do you present a gift or receive one?
5. What do people call birthdays in the target country? Are they celebrated on the birth date or on another day? How are they celebrated? Is there a special greeting to be given to someone on his or her birthday? Is there a special birthday song?

UNIT IX: At the Post Office

1. Many post offices abroad provide a much wider range of services than does the American post office. Find out what services you should expect to find available in the post office of the host country. Find out the equivalents in the target language for any postal needs you anticipate.
2. In countries where the telephone is a luxury, letter writing has a much more important role than in the U.S. Find out when a letter is necessary, desirable, or unnecessary. Learn a standard form for writing letters.
3. Find out how to use the telephone in your host country. Do you need a special coin to operate phones on the street? What are appropriate ways of answering a telephone or initiating a conversation? How do you close a conversation?
4. Someone you meet abroad may tell you to "stop by and visit sometime." Investigate the meaning of this and similarly imprecise invitations.

5. All cultures have systems for interrupting others—through language, gestures, eye contact, etc. Supposing you are in a hurry, how can you appropriately interrupt someone in the target culture? Does the system vary in accordance with sex, age, intimacy of relationship, etc.?

6. Do you know the population of your hometown, state, and country, and can you express these linguistically to your hosts in a way they can understand? How do your hosts pronounce the same names? What about other internationally known names, such as movie actors, political figures, athletes, etc.?

9

Cultural Orientation in the English as a Second Language Classroom

Janet Gaston

In The Experiment's English as a Second Language program, there is a strong emphasis placed on the learning of language within the context of culture. We see language as an expression of the way in which a particular group of people think, act, and believe; therefore, learning about a culture increases one's understanding and ability to use the language of that culture. We attempt to help our students develop ways of learning about the culture while they are in the process of learning the language.

The three exercises given below are examples of activities developed for cross-cultural orientation use in multinational ESL classes. Because our international students are already living and studying in a culture different from their own, the focus of our work is less on preparation for entering a new situation and more on adaptation to their present living/studying environment.

Observation

Purpose:
- to establish the difference between observation and judgment
- to begin to realize that what we observe is affected by what our past experiences have been (e.g., our own culture, family, education, interests)
- to realize that generalizations can be dangerous, unfair, and limiting (e.g., "All Americans are rich.")

Procedure:
1. Have students make a list of 4-6 observations they have made about their living/studying environment. It might be helpful to give examples of what you mean (food, dress, nonverbal behavior, etc.).
2. Write the observations on a blackboard or some place where everyone can see them.
3. Define with the group the difference between observation and judgment.
4. Then reexamine the observations the students have made to determine which are observations and which are judgments. Some will be very hard to determine. Do not spend a lot of time trying to put statements in one category or the other. Rather, help the students understand why some of the statements might be considered judgments. Try to change some of the obvious judgment statements to observation statements.
5. Follow with a discussion of such questions as
   - What influences the things we observe? (e.g., interests, emotions, past experience)
   - Why are observation skills important to have?
   - How can these skills be improved?

Stereotypes

Purpose:
- to look at stereotypes individuals hold
- to begin to understand how and why they are formed
- to realize that they are often invalid and lead to misunderstandings and blocks in communication

Procedure:

1. Ask each person to write down the first 3-5 things he or she thinks of when each country represented in the class is mentioned.
2. Write these things on the board or collect them and type them up for use in class the next day.
3. Give students time to read all of them.
4. Ask them to respond to what was written about their countries.
5. Follow with a discussion of such questions as
   - Why did you write the things you did?
   - Where have your ideas about different countries come from?
   - Have your stereotypes of people from different countries changed/been reinforced since you have been in the United States? Why?

Procedure:

1. Have the students list 3-6 stereotypes or preconceived ideas they had about the United States before they came here.
2. Put them on the board and look for similarities. Ask for observations related to the list.
3. Ask students where their ideas came from. Also ask if their ideas have changed since they have been in the country. Why?
4. Possibly the next day, ask a group of 3-4 Americans to come into the class and respond to these perceptions that others have of the United States.

10

Using Critical Incidents

Donald Batchelder

It is probably fair to state that students *do* regard language acquisition as an important skill and are willing to devote time and effort to learning the language of the host country. They recognize the importance of language as a communication skill and are genuinely concerned about their capacity to communicate and understand. At the same time, it might be fair to suggest that many of the same students do *not* regard other important cross-cultural elements as skill areas at all: observing, listening, information gathering, problem solving, cultural awareness, self-awareness, and human-relations skills in general.

In order to address this problem directly and to supplement other forms of orientation, The Experiment began employing the critical-incident model as a device to help the students become conscious of the field-learning process. We identified several specific variables to be worked with and provided participants with opportunities to test out these skills and work with them in practice prior to departure. The variables regarded as crucial are: (1) self-awareness, (2) communication skills, (3) problem-solving skills, (4) learning skills, (5) technical and factual background, and (6) social and cultural awareness. Our purpose is to encourage each participant in the cultural-learning process. The overall goal is the conscious development of the attitudes, approaches, and skills necessary to be a successful cultural sojourner in the host country and a self-sustaining learner in the context of another culture. One way of accomplishing this goal is through critical incidents.

No one has ever been particularly comfortable with the term "critical incident," since it carries with it a note of calamity and seems tilted toward the negative. One Experiment resident study-abroad director called it "Cultural Analysis," and another, in Guatemala, called them "Awareness Episodes." The process is the same.

The traditional college or high school course delivers materials which are already organized to a considerable extent: books, outlines, study guides, lectures, syllabi, regular evaluation and testing, and a review process. The field-learning experience away from the traditional campus floods the participant with information, new experience, change, ambiguities, and impressions. The cultural sojourner is forced, to some degree, to organize all of this into some coherent pattern personally and has to be able to integrate both cognitive and affective information. In this dynamic field situation the most needed learning habits are those of observation, reflection, organization, and conceptualization. Written communication is one way to achieve this through the mechanism and discipline of writing down succinctly one's knowledge of culture and self, posing questions for oneself, searching for answers, and noting whatever changes the experience offers or brings about in terms of attitudes, values, beliefs, behaviors, interests, and approaches.

The following cross-cultural skill areas have been taken from the excellent work of John Duley.[1] The explanations to the student which accompany each item begin with Duley's own definitions and have been expanded for use by our own students and programs.

1. Information source development. The ability to use many information sources within a social or cultural environment. The student should work to develop information-gathering skills such as observing, questioning the people one meets, and listening carefully.

2. Cultural understanding. Awareness and understanding of values, feelings, and attitudes of people in another culture, and the ways in which these influence behavior. Or, reversing it, observation of behaviors and defining the values and attitudes which undergird the behaviors.

3. Interpersonal communication. Listening well, speaking clearly, and paying attention to the expression of nonverbal communication, such as the messages delivered through physical movements, eyes, facial expressions, and the whole range of ways to transfer meaning developed through face-to-face encounter.

4. Commitment to persons and relationships. The ability to become involved deeply with people beyond superficial relationships, giving and inspiring trust and confidence, establishing a basis for mutual liking and respect, caring enough for them, and acting in ways which are both truthful for you and sensitive toward the feelings of others.

5. Decision making. The ability to come to conclusions based on your assessment of the information available and to take action. This might also be called problem solving, which includes learning to be explicit about the problem, to work out steps to a solution, and to generate alternatives. In the cross-cultural situation it is important to be able to identify what is at issue, the dimensions of the problem, and alternatives which are both personally and culturally acceptable.

6. Self-understanding. Awareness of and insight into your own learning processes (strengths, weaknesses, successes, failures, biases, values, goals, and emotions), and consciousness of self (the way you are, your own openness to looking honestly at yourself). This is particularly important in situations where conflict might exist, for example, in your tolerance for ambiguity and change, or when demands are made on you from outside. Self-understanding is important to your capacity to deal with criticism or hostility, to hear what other people are telling you, and balance that with what you tell yourself.

7. Self-reliance. Independence, resiliency, autonomy, willingness to accept responsibility for your own actions, behavior, and education. Your receptiveness to new experiences and ideas, confidence in yourself, and the ability to function independently.

These categories are handed out to the students at the start of the process, and the assignment is explained in detail. The students are then asked, during the orientation period, to select for analysis one particular episode or event which occurred just before leaving home to come to the orientation site, or perhaps something which happened en route. The assignment can be structured as follows:

1. Identify the event or occurrence with as much specificity as possible, the problem to be solved, the issue involved, etc.
2. Describe the relevant details and circumstances surrounding the event so that readers will understand what happened. (What? When? How? Why? Where?)
3. List the people involved; describe them and their relationships to you and to one another. (Who?)
4. Describe your own role in the situation (i.e., what you did, how you acted) and identify the particular cross-cultural skill or skills involved. How well or badly did you understand the situation? How well or badly did you handle the situation? How well or badly did you use the skill involved? What would you do differently the next time? Describe your interpretation of events.
5. Write a brief analysis of the incident, tell what you learned from the experience, and state your estimate of the level of development of your particular cross-cultural skills as you reflect on the incident.

Papers should be refined down to one page. The clarification involved in articulating the entire episode and its sequel in one page has proved helpful to many students in improving their writing skills, in addition to helping them become more familiar with cross-cultural concepts and actions. A staff member, advisor, or facilitator should read the papers and provide written or oral feedback promptly, prior to the next assignment. The second practice assignment during an orientation period is focused on an event or episode which occurs at the training or orientation site. Again, review and feedback are provided promptly, and, with the students' permission, the papers may be used for group discussion during subsequent orientation meetings. The general effect is to heighten the consciousness of the participants and groups to cross-cultural issues, increasing the likelihood that they thoughtfully will share learning episodes which might otherwise pass unnoticed. If time permits, a third critical-incident or cultural-awareness assignment can be given, this time leaving the choice of topic and time of occurrence completely in the hands of the students. Or, if a particularly good cross-cultural film is being used during the orientation, students may be asked to write a one-page paper describing their cultural learning or a specific cross-cultural insight derived from viewing the film.

The stage is then set for the writing of short papers during homestay abroad. The participants have developed some skill with the process, plus confidence and interest in it. There is an opportunity for the leader or advisor overseas to review and discuss the papers and, if and when group meetings are held, the papers can become the basis for some excellent cross-cultural discussions. In this manner, a mechanism for ongoing orientation is built in to the structure of the overseas program. Instead of sharing their five best colored slides, they begin to share their most illuminating learning experiences with each other and the leader or advisor.

Notes:
1. John Duley. "Cross-Cultural Field Study." In *Implementing Field Experience Education*, New Directions for Higher Education, no. 6 (San Francisco: Jossey-Bass, 1974), 13-23.

11

Cultural Adjustment, Power, and Personal Ethics: Three Critical Incidents

Karen Blanchard

When a sojourner enters a new culture, to which culture of the many that make up almost every nation does she or he adjust? Which behaviors, of the range encountered, are adapted to? Which rules of interaction are followed? The ability to answer these questions with some degree of sophistication assumes the need for more than a superficial understanding of the culture.

Questions of this nature are most often raised when the sojourner is faced with an ethical dilemma, for example, when watching an old woman being shoved aside so another passenger can board a bus or seeing a man hitting a woman or a woman hitting a child. Are these manifestations of cultural norms to which one should adapt, or is one seeing abnormal behavior to be shunned? Would members of the dominant culture expect this behavior of a visitor? Would people belonging to one of the nondominant cultures expect visitors to behave in this manner?

These kinds of situations are consciously perceived by the sojourners. There are other situations, however, of which the visitor or foreign resident may not be aware. For example, one may learn words in the language of the country which demean people of another culture or linguistic group. In the United States, what does a foreign visitor of color understand when he or she is told to ask for "flesh"-colored bandages?

Much of the literature about, and many of the approaches to, intercultural interaction have focused on developing the knowledge, skills, and awareness essential to adjusting to a new cultural environment. In great part, that thrust has been a response to the myriad miscommunications, both dangerous and benign, that occur when sojourners consciously or unconsciously demand that the new culture adjust to *them*, i.e., be like their culture.

While this kind of learning and skill development is essential for effective intercultural interaction, it is important to look more deeply at the adjustment process and ask challenging and thought-provoking questions. Doing so inevitably forces us to face the problem of consciously aligning our actions with our conclusions. As we grasp the fact that cultures are not monolithic—that in every major geopolitical unit of the world there are a dominant culture and cocultures; lesser or greater differences between one set of people and another; wide variations to be found in goals, values, and expectations—we are confronted by what adjustment may mean in terms of our own ethics and values.

One useful avenue for looking at that issue is to understand the idea of dominance within cultures and how it might inform and change a sojourner's response to the adjustment and intercultural interaction processes. In other words, we may well want to ask: is *not* adjusting an appropriate response in an intercultural setting?

Edith Folb writes:

> ...when we talk about the concept of dominant culture, we are really talking about power—those who dominate culture, those who historically or traditionally have had the most persistent and far-reaching impact on culture, on what we think and say, on what we believe and do in our society.... Dominant culture, therefore, significantly reflects the precepts and artifacts of those who dominate culture and is not necessarily, or even usually, a reference to numbers, but to power.[1]

One view of the state of the world today, using the newly dismembered Soviet Union and Yugoslavia and the riots in the United States as examples, might be to say that change and violence are a result of the concept of one culture (dominant) being pushed to recognize what has always been there: unrecognized (nondominant) cultures wanting to share power. With that in mind, a sojourner may want to ask: What has been written on how to communicate effectively with people from those particular cultures? What has been written and who wrote that information (taking into consideration that those who dominate culture are in influential positions) often define the cultural behaviors about which a sojourner reads and upon which she or he is expected to act. How does this larger context influence the way a sojourner views, communicates, and acts in those cultures and, in turn, is viewed and responded to by people from those cultures? Dominance is one of the lenses through which cultures and, therefore, appropriate adjusting responses, need to be examined.

In my course discussions at the School for International Training (SIT) on these issues, I have found that those individuals who have difficulty describing their cultural backgrounds are most often from dominant cultural groups, regardless of country of origin. Although they may be desirous of change, they tend to take their dominant cultural background for granted as the norm. Conversely, those individuals from nondominant cultures are usually conscious that various cultures exist within a context and are most aware of the nuances in their cultural backgrounds.

How do we prepare ourselves and others—from both dominant and nondominant cultures—to question the process of cross-cultural adjustment in such a way that the foundations for developing nonexploitative relationships are maintained and valued? I will refer you to a few of the exercises and ideas in this book which I, and the participants with whom I have worked, have found effective.

I start out using Lise Sparrow's Cultural Autobiography exercise from her article, "Examining Cultural Identity" (this volume). Having requested that the students complete the autobiography as called for, I then ask participants, in triads, to think of ways that their ethnicity and class have provided them with both strengths and challenges (two ways each for both ethnicity and class, or more if time allows).

Once that is completed, I ask them to share with one another how ethnicity and class may have affected their interactions with others and others' interactions with them and to be ready to describe their insights to the large group. If done at the beginning of a training program or class, this effectively sets the stage for further discussion of adjustment issues.

In the context of the "Seven Concepts" training design described by Gochenour and Janeway earlier in this book, stages three, four, and five are particularly appropriate places in the design to draw out the issues which emerge from the Cultural Autobiography exercise. Dealing with them in a gradual progression has been most effective for the groups with whom I have worked.

The critical incidents found at the end of this article were created by participants in the graduate Program in Intercultural Management at SIT. They have been used in my course on intercultural communication as part of a class on ethics and communication. When used prior to a class session or discussion of oppression theory and dominant culture, I have found them to be particularly useful.

I believe that it is important for us to look at what personal adjustment really means in an intercultural setting. We need to explore and discuss what we are adjusting to and to see when adjustment or accommodation is appropriate and when it is not. We need to understand the relationship between adjusting and our own values. The deeper we perceive that process, the more we are likely to understand one another better and contribute to the field of intercultural communication and, I hope, to a more peaceful world.

Critical Incident I

There are significant health problems in general on this isolated Pacific atoll, where there is one rudimentary health-care facility staffed by a poorly trained nurse. It is part of traditional island culture for the people of Butaritari to bury their dead on the family living compound within the overcrowded village communities. Due to the burgeoning population, land within the village is scarce, but the deceased are continuing to be buried according to tradition, meaning they are being buried closer to the compound's wells (the only dependable source of fresh water on the island), causing serious health problems. The island priest (an Australian expatriate) has said that he has repeatedly warned the people of the consequences of burying their dead family members near the water sources but has made no other attempts to use his authority to discourage this traditional practice. As mentioned, there are significant health problems on the island and endemic diarrhea among the island children; death resulting from these water-borne diseases is not uncommon. A UN volunteer-hydrologist has come to the island and has determined that the water in some areas around these compounds is indeed contaminated. You are part of the village community, living and working there as a volunteer for an extended period of time.

Critical Incident II

You are a social worker employed by a social service agency in a midwestern city. Your responsibility is to be the case manager for the single-parent, female-headed families in the local Kampuchean (Cambodian) community.

The Kampuchean community numbers about four hundred people. Each family in this community has had at least one member, and usually more, killed in Kampuchea by American bombs or by the horrors of the Pol Pot regime. Almost all of the families have come to your community with literally little more than the shirts on their backs and accompanied by their remaining relatives. These refugees, especially the children, are a central source of identity and meaning for community members.

You and your agency have become concerned about the living conditions of the Kampuchean families, and most especially about the single-parent, female-headed families. Almost all of the latter share some characteristics. They live in rat-infested, deteriorating housing, yet are wary of moving into what they perceive as drug-infested public housing. During the last year three Kampuchean children contracted lead poisoning. The mothers, almost without exception, cannot read, write, or speak English passably. In addition, the mothers universally suffer from depression. Migraine headaches, sleeplessness, and acute physical aches and pains are a daily reality for these women. Almost all of the families are dependent upon welfare. Your efforts to encourage them to learn English and get a job are often met with the response, "I do not want to leave my children."

Critical Incident III

You are training, in-country, to become a community-development worker. Cross-cultural sensitivity is a component of the training program. During one of these sessions you are made aware of some cultural norms and practices and how your organization would like you to respond to them.

You are told that one common practice in this country is wife beating. You are advised to not get involved in any such incident that you may witness. This practice is seen as quite normal, and any interference, especially since you are an outsider, would be seen as terribly inappropriate. At best, you would likely get no support from others nearby, and at worst, you may invoke a very negative or hostile response.

Training is now over and you have been at post for several months. You live in half a house, and in the other half is a local family. On many a night you have been kept awake by the loud, and often heated, arguments of the couple next door. You have also noticed occasional bruises and swellings on the face of the wife.

It is early Wednesday morning. At 2:00 A.M. you are suddenly awakened by raucous voices. You hear some loud noises and the wife is crying and pleading with her husband to stop. The wife runs out into the yard and her husband follows. The argument and the physical abuse continue.

The reading of each critical incident may be followed by a consideration of the same set of questions:

1. Is anything "right" or "wrong" in this situation? Do you need more information?
2. What would you do in this situation?
3. What influenced your decision?
4. What questions would you ask yourself in making ethical decisions regardless of the situation?

Notes:
1.   Edith Folb, "Who's Got Room at the Top? Issues of Dominance and Nondominance in Intracultural Communication." In *Intercultural Communication: A Reader*, 4th ed., 1985, edited by Larry A. Samovar and Richard E. Porter (Belmont, CA: Wadsworth), 119-27.

12

Exercises for Building Intercultural Skills

A Note on Bird Names

The next four exercises carry names which hardly explain what the activities are about. In fact, their titles bear little or no relationship to anything sober, sensible, and pedagogical. The reason for this is that the oldest of the exercises, The Albatross, had that name obscurely given to it sometime in the distant past. It arrived already ladened with its title—complete with jokes among participants about how it hung about their necks. Those of us at The Experiment who were interested in simulations and experiential exercises felt that there might be some poetic justice in continuing the tradition. So, when the "X-ians" came into existence, pretty soon the exercises had to have a bird name, thus The Owl. Similarly, it seemed easier to call The Mockingbird by that name than to think up something more descriptive. When Claude Pepin developed his exercise using blindfolds, what could have been more appropriate than to call it The Ostrich? (Editor)

The Mockingbird
Theodore Gochenour

This is a short exercise which can be used for almost any number of people at one time. It is useful as an "ice breaker," though its point goes beyond that to one of raising the issue of cultural distance, demonstrating (particularly for Americans and Canadians) that the physical/emotional reality of relating to another person at an unfamiliar, close distance may be harder to accept than the concept itself.

I. Setting Up the Exercise

Materials — Something to eat, preferably unfamiliar to the participants, or at least not usual. Two different things to eat are needed, each sufficient for half of those taking part in the exercise. Since one virtue of the exercise is brevity, it is best to choose food items which can be easily and quickly passed out to the participants and held in the hand without undue mess.

Sequence of the Exercise — Ask the participants to form two lines, each person standing back-to-back with another person in the other line. This enables those conducting the exercise to pass out two kinds of food easily by passing down the two rows and handing out the food to each person—one row receiving one food item, the second row the other item.

When the food has been passed out

and each person is holding his or her item, instruct the two rows to turn so that each person is now facing the person who was originally in a back-to-back position. The group is instructed to stand toe-to-toe, literally, and to eat the food passed out and discuss it with the person each is facing.

Allow two or three minutes for conversation, perhaps up to five minutes if desired. Then announce that the exercise is over.

Note: This exercise can also be done nonverbally by having each partner, while standing toe-to-toe, communicate about what each is eating without speaking. Also, concern about the transmission of infection may be alleviated by using portions of food with tongs, serving food that has been thoroughly cooked, and/or describing measures that have been taken to assure that the food is safe.

II. Discussion

Given the introductory nature of the exercise, an extended discussion may not be necessary or desired.

Participants should be asked what reactions they felt during the exercise—whether they found it easy to maintain the toe-to-toe stance or tended to step back. The person conducting the exercise should have made an effort to observe the various behaviors occurring as the exercise took place. Most likely, he or she will have noted several patterns of physical reaction to the close distance: tendency to twist to one side or lean back, awkwardness with hands, etc. These observations should be shared with the group as the discussions develop.

If there are both men and women in the group, some pairs doing the exercise will be men-men, some women-women, and some mixed. These variations should provide some useful points of observation and discussion.

In concluding the discussion, the point should be emphasized that our concept of cultural distance is something which we can understand on one level, but may not be able to physically and emotionally deal with quite as readily. This awareness should be extended to other aspects of cultural interaction.

The Ostrich
Claude Pepin

Here's an idea for preparing individuals about to enter a cross-cultural experience, one that looks at those first few moments in an unfamiliar setting. Many of us know the feeling: sitting in a train station with new sensations pouring in—language, architecture, smells, music, dress—some exciting, some foreboding and most unfamiliar. First, thoughts and feelings turn to personal needs: Where will I sleep tonight? I'm hungry! Where's the W.C.? How do I get from here to wherever? In those first few moments, these random, albeit important, needs often hinder our ability to see clearly and enjoy our new surroundings. The following exercise helps individuals become more aware of the importance of nonverbal behavior and may help them profit further from initial contact with a new culture.

Clear the furniture from a room and blindfold a group of ten to fifteen people; whisper a separate number in each person's ear. Instruct the group to line up in ascending numerical order without speaking. There is no time limit, but the group should indicate nonverbally when the task has been completed.

Our purpose is to have participants experience the feeling of having an intense need to communicate something they consider of extreme importance and being unable to do so. The blindfold and nonverbal limitation represent communication barriers such as language; the number represents food, lodging, and other needs. The blindfold symbolizes those elements to which we are blind in new experiences. Participants in this exercise are bound to feel frustration and become impatient, as is the case when we encounter communication barriers. But the task can only be completed if participants accept barriers and learn to deal with this novel situation. Similarly, in the train station we would hope to accustom ourselves to new sights, smells, and sounds; accept a new pace of action; learn some new words; greet people as is their custom—in short, tune in to the new cultural and linguistic surroundings—rather than desperately attempting to get someone to listen to our needs for food, lodging, and directions. Getting a feeling for the new environment is a first step toward understanding it.

During the discussion, participants can share their thoughts about the experience itself ("What was it like to be blindfolded? To have to communicate without saying words?") and analyze their reactions ("What was difficult? How did you deal with it? What did you enjoy? Have you ever had similar sensations in other situations?"). It is important to link the blindfold/nonverbal exercise to the cross-cultural experience they are about to enter. The discussion should center on what participants have learned from the experience and how they might apply this learning to their first few moments in a new situation.

The Albatross
Theodore Gochenour

If you have never taken part in The Albatross exercise, it would be best to do so before you decide whether it is useful for your training and orientation purposes.

There are two parts to the exercise. The first part consists of performing a ceremonial greeting between members of an imaginary culture (Albatross) and foreigners (those participants being trained or oriented). There should be no onlookers. The second part consists of an extended discussion. Albatross is an experiential learning device of some power, but it is relatively useless unless the discussion is treated with particular thoughtfulness and attention.

I. Setting Up the Exercise

Albatross seems best done in small groups of twelve to fifteen. If possible, participants should include a more or less equal number of men and women. A circle of chairs is arranged—enough for the male participants, with one chair placed in the circle a bit prominently for the use of the Albatrossian man.

Materials	Dishes or bowls for: (1) hand washing, (2) liquid to drink, and (3) food to eat. Sheets or other cloth for the use of the Albatrossian man and woman, candles, incense, or other extras as desired.
Sequence of the Exercise	It is important to realize that there is no set sequence or necessary pattern to follow. It may be best to create your own variations on the directions below to meet special situations, such as having too many participants, or all of

one sex, etc. With that in mind, what follows is an outline of the standard way Albatross is run. There are other sequences which have been or can be developed. The characteristics of the selected sequence are less important than having clear objectives and valid reasons for using that sequence.

The degree to which participants are prepared and briefed is a matter of choice. Generally it is best to offer a minimum of information prior to the exercise. "You're going to go into the room for a cultural exercise" should be enough for most training situations. It is not good to tell participants to look for this or that, to make sure they observe carefully, or cause them to be self-consciously expecting to be judged in some way. Albatross works best when participants enter the room without much idea at all as to what is going to take place. Their reactions will reflect the participants as they are and will be the source of the learning which potentially can be gained from the exercise.

A male and female Albatrossian are in their places, the man on the chair, the woman kneeling beside him. Participants are brought or directed into the circle of chairs, females with shoes off and males with shoes on. The Albatrossian couple are draped in white sheets and otherwise made up to look exotic and unfamiliar, the woman without shoes, the man with shoes.

The first activity (which can be done before the greetings or combined with them) is for the Albatrossians (mainly the man) to attempt to induce the female participants off any chairs they may happen to be sitting on and to get them down on the floor, and to induce male participants to do the reverse. This effort, and all other communications during the exercise, are in a special Albatrossian language. Albatrossians are sedate, reserved, gentle, and loving people who do not manhandle their guests. Touching is only done in ceremonial ways, such as in the greetings. Thus, the effort to get the participants into proper place is done principally through (1) a hiss, which indicates disapproval, (2) an appreciative hum, which indicates approval, or (3) a clicking of the tongue, which serves for all sorts of attention getting, transfer of factual information, etc.

The next activity is the circle of greetings. The Albatrossian man gets up and goes around the circle greeting in turn each male participant, who stands up to receive the greeting. The Albatrossian man holds each male participant by the shoulders and waist, then rubs their right legs together across the calves. After being greeted, the visitor should sit back down in his chair. Then the Albatrossian woman gets up and goes around the circle greeting in turn each female participant, who also stands. She kneels in front of the female guest and runs both hands down the lower legs and feet in a ceremonious way. Each female participant then resumes a kneeling position.

After the greetings, a pause ensues during which all simply wait. The Albatrossians always maintain unsmiling (but serene and pleasant) expressions and do not register in facial reactions their feelings or responses to what may go on in the circle. Visitors who giggle or talk or otherwise disturb the ritual are hissed at, but not with anger.

A bowl of water is next brought around the circle by the Albatrossian woman. Beginning with the Albatrossian man, each male in the circle dips the fingers of his right hand into the bowl and lifts or waves the hand gracefully to dry it. The women's hands are not washed. The Albatrossian woman returns to her place for a few minutes before beginning the next activity.

She then—upon a clicking cue from the man—rises and offers food to each male in turn, beginning with the Albatrossian man. She sticks her hands into the food and stuffs a little into each mouth. Upon being fed the Albatrossian man indicates his appreciation by a loud hum or moan (which can be accompanied by rubbing his stomach). While the male participants are being fed, the Albatrossian man tries to indicate by example how they should express their appreciation with proper moans and stomach rubbing. After the men are fed, the Albatrossian woman next feeds each woman in turn. Then she returns to her kneeling position beside the Albatrossian man.

During these pauses, which should be prolonged for effect, the Albatrossian man gently pushes the woman's head downward from time to time as she kneels. The Albatrossian couple may communicate with each other with clicks or other noises. They maintain a steady ceremoniousness, doing nothing hurriedly or carelessly.

Next follows the serving of drink. In the same manner, the Albatrossian woman first gives the cup to the Albatrossian man to drink from, then circles among the male participants. Next she goes round the circle to the female participants before returning to her place and resuming her kneeling posture.

After another pause, the two Albatrossians rise and proceed around the circle of guests, communicating with each other through the customary clicking sounds. Without making obvious indications to the participants, they select the female guest with the largest feet. That participant is then led over to the Albatrossian chair. The female participant—like the Albatrossian woman—is induced to kneel beside the chair.

The last activity of the ceremony is a repeat of the greeting. The Albatrossian man rises and makes the rounds of the circle, greeting each male participant. He is followed by the Albatrossian woman, greeting each woman in turn. At that point, the two Albatrossians indicate to the selected participant left kneeling by the chair that she should follow them out. The three people leave the circle, concluding the first part of the exercise.

Note: Participants in the 1990s are likely to have legitimate concern about the possible transfer of infection by a hand traveling from one mouth to another. A simple change in the procedures for food and drink can be made to meet this concern. For example, the Albatrossian woman could feed each guest a separate cracker, using tongs which never touch the lips. A substitute for drink could be a pile of washed and wet leaves. For each participant the Albatrossian woman ceremonially shakes a separate wet leaf on the lips of the participant, then drops it to the floor.

Ideally, the items of food and drink should be "strange," i.e., something which looks and tastes odd or unusual, perhaps even a little unsavory. This is a way of emphasizing one of the underlying objectives of the exercise: to create a simulated cultural situation which feels unfamiliar but convincing.

II. Cultural Assumptions and Rationale

As elaborated later, part of the point of The Albatross exercise is to provide an opportunity for people to learn by observation, to infer meaning from the totality of what happened, to make some insightful guesses as to what the Albatrossian culture may be like. Since this cultural-observation aspect is important, it is best to conduct the exercise with as much consistency as possible, particularly if there are several ceremonial circles being run concurrently by different pairs of Albatrossians. There should be a cultural frame of reference agreed on by all Albatrossian performers. This prevents the discussion which follows the exercise from getting bogged down into differences which might take place in the way one Albatrossian couple performed the ceremony compared with another. The more all Albatrossians involved perform consistently, the easier it is to keep the discussion focused on what is significant. Following are some of the standard cultural assumptions which usually are in play and which the participants have the problem of figuring out as the exercise unfolds.

Though the exercise is deliberately set up to indicate otherwise to an American audience, in fact the Albatrossian society values women above men. Earth is sacred; all fruitfulness is blessed; those (women) who bring life into being are one with Earth, and only they are able (by virtue of their inherent qualities) to walk directly upon the ground. Thus, men must wear shoes, and their greeting does not deal with Earth. The woman's greeting emphasizes the ground and feet. Only women are able to prepare and offer the fruits of Earth.

The roles of men and women in the society reflect this relationship to Earth, though to the new observer it may appear as if other meanings are present. For example, the fact that the Albatrossian man pushes down the head of the kneeling Albatrossian woman is a fulfilling of his obligations in the society. It is his duty to remind her of sacredness, to approach it through her, to protect her from forgetfulness. He drinks and eats first to save her and all that she represents from harm or defilement.

Albatrossians have a language, though only some part of it is required or used in the greeting ceremony (the clicks, hums, hisses). It may be useful to approach the language question with another assumption: that Albatrossians communicate via mental telepathy, and the few sounds they use are mainly a means of getting a person's attention.

The society values calm, serenity, stateliness. The Albatrossians are peaceful, welcoming of strangers, generous, loving, and tolerant. They eat and drink things which they like (though they may not be to the taste of foreign visitors). Their patterns of life and their ceremonies (such as the greeting ceremony) are time-honored and are considered to be self-evidently correct and adequate.

This last is important. Albatrossians must bear in mind (and participants will realize later in discussion) that what is, *is*. Albatrossians are no different from any other people in making the unconscious assumption that they are entirely normal. Thus, they assume that the visitors *want* to be greeted in the customary Albatrossian manner, that the visitor knows as well as they what is correct (though they are tolerant and gentle in correcting lapses), that choosing the woman with the largest feet among the participants is *necessary*, etc.

The ceremony is that of greeting visitors—it is not to be implied that it is the totality of the society. For example, a church service in the U.S. is both a bona fide segment of cultural behavior and yet not indicative of everything in that culture. Performers of The Albatross may wish to create various philosophical or behavioral rationales, but usually the foregoing are more or less sufficient. During the discussion following the exercise, any inconsistencies in performance or tricky questions can always be explained as tribal differences.

But it is important for those performing as Albatrossians to make the jump into a different culture within themselves. The Albatrossian culture does not need to be explained or justified. One should attempt to enter into a spirit of "suchness," i.e., that an Albatrossian is as much a whole, self-evident, implicitly assumed person as is an American. You are not putting on a show. Through you a culture is expressing itself in one of its customary ways.

III. Discussion

This is the most important part of the exercise. There are basically two broad levels obtainable in The Albatross exercise. The first is the cultural-observation level. The exercise gives participants a chance to test their powers of observation, to infer correct behavior from nonverbal or indirect clues, and to get some idea (at least a beginning one) of what the Albatross society is like. The second broad level is one of self-awareness—of participants being given a chance to assess their own reactions and feelings and thereby to add to their self-knowledge.

Since participants are full of their own reactions after an Albatross exercise, it is best to structure the discussion on this pattern:

Collect ideas on "where they have been," i.e., what happened, what sort of activity they were engaged in. This develops into a generally agreed understanding that they have had contact with some kind of "culture." This is more than a perfunctory introduction to the discussion. The reason for exploring ideas on the nature of what happened—letting these arise without either immediate confirmation or denial—is that it tells the discussion leader much about the group at hand and its state of being.

Then the discussion can move on to what was objectively observed. Collect all possible impressions: "they did this" or "their language is...." It is helpful to ask participants to screen out for the moment their own feelings about the culture and, later, to tell what happened to them personally.

This part of the discussion will get into whether Albatross (the name can be used at any time or not, as desired) is a land where women are oppressed, "a sexist society," etc. It is best to let all ideas flow if possible and not supply answers. Likewise, it is best if contrary views can arise from within the group rather than from the leader. Eventually, someone will question the assumption of male superiority, and the discussion leader can build upon it naturally.

In this area of cultural observation, the major points which need to be brought out are: how our observations are colored by our own cultural assumptions; how well or poorly we observe what happens to us (do we notice details or pay close attention?); that we can, in fact, infer a lot of useful information from what we observe and learn what is expected of us without being told in so many words; and that things don't always mean what they seem. Thus, this part of the discussion consists of sharing information and offering participants the opportunity to think about their own skills in observation. At some juncture it will be valuable to make the additional point clear that many, if not most, of the observations offered by participants will be highly value laden. Here again, one of the participants will eventually point this out, and the leader needs to be alert to see that the idea is heard and digested by the whole group.

In this area of observation, there will usually be a strong tendency among the participants to want answers from the discussion leader: "Why did they do...?" "Do all Albatrossians...?" The goal here should be to try to get responses to such questions *from the group itself*, varied ones, contradictory ones, some of which at the appropriate moment the discussion leader can confirm or suggest be taken as probably right or as a hypothesis. The leader should try to help the group see that questions such as "Do all Albatrossians...?" are inherently meaningless in light of their own common sense and cultural experience. Finally, the leader should be alert for ways to help participants understand the limitations of such "why" questions. This means that "Why do Albatrossians do such and such?" followed by "Albatrossians do such and such because of..." simply confirms participants in a limiting pattern of thinking. While some questions might be given "here's why" answers, the leader should aim toward creating the awareness that the "why's" of human behavior do not usually lend themselves to simple, neat (sociological/anthropological) concepts and answers.

When the purely informational elements begin to get exhausted, it is good to move the discussion clearly into the area of personal feelings and reactions. Usually it is not difficult to get middle-ground reactions, "I got tired of sitting...," or "interesting...." It may take prodding to get participants to express stronger opinions and reactions, positive or negative. The thing is to try to help participants see that their own reactions are very relative, that next to them is sitting someone with a contrary reaction. In other words, a good discussion leader takes opportunities as they arise to enable participants to see that the exercise is not good or bad or boring or any other categorical label. Rather, the exercise per se is none of these things, but takes on this or that character from being seen through a pair of personal glasses. The basic idea is to let any and all reactions be expressed, yet to develop the awareness in each participant that he or she is essentially responsible for what "happened."

As participants often do not like their own reactions and behaviors, inevitably the comments arise that "if the exercise were done differently..." or "had it not been an artificial situation, I would

have...." Sometimes this question of artificiality arises from a participant who had no adverse reactions, but who wants to offer advice on
how the exercise can be improved.

The question of artificiality is central to the insights and increased
self-awareness the exercise offers. The leader must make it clear that
The Albatross exercise was artificial insofar as it was a simulation. It
was not artificial in the aspect which matters most: that during a
given period of time, a group of people did such and such in that
room and each participant had real reactions. It is up to the participant to admit that whatever those reactions (and behaviors) were,
they *happened*, and that essentially it is immaterial how "well" or how
"realistically" the exercise was run. It may help to run it realistically
and with theatrical skill (for the benefits to be gained from the
cultural-observation level), but as *an event in the lives of the participants*, it was as real as anything which may happen to them.

This insight, if it can be gained, is valuable. It will seem self-
evident to some and totally meaningless or alien to others, but the
leader should try. In doing so it helps to point out to the participants
that Albatross is a device which one can personally use to look at
oneself. Each person knows how he or she responded. It is up to each
person to realize that (1) those reactions occurred and were real, (2)
whatever it was that caused those reactions, the individual has
responsibility for them, and (3) there is no right or wrong to the
exercise. It means whatever each person's inward awareness causes
it to mean.

The Owl
Theodore Gochenour

I. Setting

This exercise consists of a short (approximately fifteen minutes) interview between two Americans and three members of another culture—Country X—followed by a brief break and a final meeting in which the Americans make a request of the "X-ians," as they are called.

Briefing the Americans. Not much time will be needed for this preliminary briefing (ten or fifteen minutes), since the objective is to have those who play the roles of Americans do so with a minimum of advance thought that could cause them to be especially observant of their own behavior. In briefing the Americans, the emphasis should be on (1) making the sequence of the role play clear, (2) conveying an awareness of what being a journalist might be like, and (3) providing some motivational push to make them want to succeed.

Briefing the X-ians. Approximately one hour will be needed here. Time will be spent in reading over the briefing sheet, then talking out the implications. The basic problem posed to those who play the X-ian roles is that of trying to get under the skin of the culture—to play their roles with a sense of naturalness—avoiding hamming it up or being obvious. X-ians need to feel that Country X is as real and believable a culture as any other. Part of the briefing time for X-ians should be devoted to practicing the roles, discussing the exercise with each other, and deciding on how they would like to refine or elaborate on it.

Five chairs should be set up to accommodate the people involved in the role play. Several may be run at the same time, depending on the number of participants in your group, though you must have one or two observers watch and be ready to discuss each of the role plays.

The facilitator should be ready to alert the American couple when it is about time to end the interview and move into the next phase of the role play, which calls for them to leave the room, confer briefly, and then return to their meeting with the X-ians.

Both parties to the role play should be strongly urged not to rely too heavily on their printed instructions, but to play their roles as freely and as spontaneously as possible. It is important that, once the role play is over and before the discussion has begun, participants not share their instructions with the other side, nor engage in conversation other than what is called for in the role play.

II. The Discussion

In discussing this exercise, it is preferable to allow time for people to express what they understand about "culture" before getting into personal reactions, feelings, etc. One dimension of the exercise is simple cross-cultural observation: how the Americans and observers perceived what was going on and how they sorted out meaning.

Thus, one way to start is by tabulating the "success" and "failure" results from each pair of Americans (assuming there was more than one group doing the role play), e.g., "How many got a yes answer?" "How many got a no?" Then ask the Americans who received no answers what they can say about the culture of X. Collect these as observed facts, without value judgments or personal reactions. When this has run its course, ask the remaining Americans (those who got yes answers) to contribute what they know about Country X.

After sharing observations and insights about Culture X, it will be time to shift to asking the Americans who got no answers why they think they were turned down. A good next step is to ask the remaining Americans why they got yes answers. This procedure brings the group to a fairly clear awareness (1) that what one person observes, another often misses and (2) that the element of behavior, of culturally sensitive interaction with the X-ians, plays a strong role in achieving success.

A next step is to ask the X-ians who said no to tell why they gave that answer and the X-ians who said yes to say why. This moves the discussion into issues of cross-cultural sensitivity and serves as a bridge into personal reactions and feelings. The discussion should explore these feelings, especially what it felt like to be an X-ian encountering Americans behaving as they did and what it felt like to be an American encountering X-ian behavior. There are a number of possible and valuable subjects to explore; e.g., the difficulty or ease of playing the X-ian role, the relationship between men and men and women and women as well as between men and women, the frustrations of language, the significance of nonverbal communication, etc.

Since this exercise hinges on male/female relationships—and, in the case of Country X, sets up a cultural relationship quite different from what is normally or traditionally encountered in the U.S.—you may wish to explore that subject at some length. Stereotyping is one possible focus. Ask how the women who played X-ians cast themselves and on what model? What was their relationship to Peh (an X-ian character in the role play) and why did they choose to play the relationship that way?

In leading the discussion, the facilitator should attempt to relate behavior, perceptions, stereotyping, and reactions to the here and now, with each participant being asked to think about his or her own experience in the role play and what it has to teach about cultural self-awareness.

III. Briefing Sheet #1

You are a member of Country X, an ancient land of high culture which, in the course of the centuries, has tended to develop along isolationist lines. X-ians have a deep and complete acceptance of a way of life which no outside influence has altered in any appreciable way for many years, due to the sense of perfection and harmony of life which X-ians derive from their culture.

In Country X, women are the natural leaders, administrators, heads of households, principal artists, owners of wealth (which is passed on via the female line), and rulers of the state. Men rarely work outside the home, where they keep house, cook, mind children, etc., and then only in menial positions where heavy labor is required. Among X-ian women, education is important, with a high percentage going on to the university level. Among men, there is little interest and no encouragement to attain more education than basic literacy. In all respects, women know themselves to be superior to men and are acknowledged to be superior by the men, both in individual attitudes and as expressed institutionally. There is a well-known expression, for example, which goes, "Don't send a man on a woman's errand."

Knowing much of the outside world, and rendered somewhat uncomfortable by what they know of male/female relationships in many other countries, X-ians have tended to withdraw into themselves. In Country X, marriage is between two women, forming what is known as The Bond. The two women (The Bond) may wish to jointly receive a man into their household, for purposes of creating children, for tending the home, etc. The two women in The Bond are equal in all respects, jointly agree in all decisions, and have mutual responsibility for a man, should he be affiliated with them. Relating to a Bond, a man is legally regarded as an entity, receiving protection from The Bond. The man is considered "cherished" by The Bond, and being cherished is considered very desirable among men.

The X-ian women are famous for their artistic powers, particularly in having developed the design and care of gardens into a unique art form. In Country X, the Queen's Garden is open once a year on her birthday to the women of the country (no men allowed) in celebration of the natural processes of growth and rebirth. No foreigners have been able, so far, to observe the Queen's Garden Festival, though there is no law which would prevent it from happening.

X-ians share with some cultures of the world a marked discomfort with prolonged eye contact. They, of course, look at another person with brief, polite glances when they are in conversation, but do not hold another person's eyes with their own. In Country X, one is careful not to stare, since it is very impolite and considered to be the worst kind of aggressiveness.

You are an X-ian Bond, Ms. Alef and Ms. Beh, with your Cherished Man Peh. Ms. Alef holds an important position in the Ministry of Foreign Affairs, as directress of Cultural Affairs. Ms. Beh holds a position also in the Ministry of Foreign Affairs as special assistant to the minister. Both women are distantly related to the queen. Cherished Man Peh has been taken along by the two women of The Bond on one of their official trips outside Country X. The three of you are now in a restaurant in Athens and have been spotted by an American couple whom you have met once before but do not know very well.

When speaking with the Americans, you must limit your vocabulary to words of only one or two syllables. The purposes for this are: (1) your native language is that of Country X, and thus it is quite understandable for you to be limited in your command of English and (2) counting syllables keeps you from glibly tossing out anthropological jargon as you try to explain the culture of Country X.

The American couple will attempt to gain your help in getting permission to observe the next Queen's Garden Festival. They will talk about general subjects with you for about fifteen minutes. At that time, on some pretext, the American couple will excuse themselves for a few minutes, then return and ask you for your help.

While they are gone, you must decide whether to say yes or no. There are three things to consider. You should decide yes if, in your judgment, the Americans have shown cultural sensitivity to what X-ians are like. This means looking for three main things:

1. The American woman must be the one asking for permission and she must ask the X-ian Bond (not Peh). The men in the role play (both the American man and Peh) must not be involved in the request.
2. You must decide how thoughtful the Americans have been about your limitations in the use of English. They should not just rattle on when it is obvious by your speech that you may not understand them very well. If they show sensitivity in this regard, it will be a factor favoring yes.
3. The Americans must also show sensitivity to your customs in eye contact. If they continue to stare at you during the conversation (and the request), then your answer would be no.

III. Briefing Sheet #2

You are two Americans, male and female, both well-known journalists. Both of you have M.A.'s in journalism from recognized schools and have spent several years in international travel and reporting on political, cultural, and artistic subjects in a number of countries.

Never at a loss to detect a possible story, you are pleased to encounter three people in a restaurant in Athens whom you have met once before briefly. You do not remember their names, but do remember that they are from Country X, a rather exotic and unusual place not often visited by foreigners. Country X is one of those places in the world about which there are more legends than facts. It is known, however, to be a society with highly developed arts, literature, and gardens (which are apparently some kind of art form), and with an atmosphere of being inaccessible and not too interested in getting into the world tourism business. One of the intriguing things about which speculation sometimes appears in the Sunday supplements is the X-ian Queen's Garden Festival, which takes place apparently once a year and which no one has ever visited or photographed. To do so, especially to be the first, would be a true journalistic coup.

In this exercise, you will approach the X-ians at their restaurant table and ask to join them. Talk with them about general subjects for about fifteen minutes. Then, find a pretext to leave the table for one or two minutes and decide together what would be the best way to approach your real subject: can you get permission to observe the next Queen's Garden Festival and do a story with pictures?

Try not to let your conversation run on too long. After you return from conferring, make your request to the X-ians. You will get a yes or no answer. At that point, the exercise is over, and you excuse yourselves again and leave.

13

The Drop-Off

Donald Batchelder

The Experiment began using The Drop-Off as an orientation and training technique in 1962, as part of a community investigation process. We were interested at the time in helping a group to field-test theoretical concepts related to the ways in which communities begin, organize themselves, and develop. Teams were sent to several Vermont towns to try to track down twenty-four separate and interrelated elements of community, which had been laid out for them in a training course developed by Desmond M. Connor.[1]

We learned that groups can discover sources of information and assemble an impressive amount of data in a short time, if prepared beforehand with a systematic inquiry approach and a theoretical framework. Beyond this, it became apparent that the participants began to learn important things about their own learning process through this field experience. The fact that many of them had to overcome an initial reluctance to approach strangers, even though they were citizens of the same country and spoke the same language, gave us a clue to other possible applications of the process. Subsequent usage and variations upon it confirmed that participants found themselves experiencing many of the same feelings and personal reactions which they would later encounter overseas in the cross-cultural situation in the host country. Intentional use of The Drop-Off as an orientation exercise for the purpose of developing self-confidence as well as field-inquiry skills became a common practice in many different programs. It has been used mainly with American students and groups here in the United States, in English, but has also been employed overseas in the language of the host country. It has also been used by students and teachers from other countries, as an introduction to community life in the United States and by mixed teams composed of foreign students and Americans.

The Experiment does not claim to have invented The Drop-Off exercise process, but we have done considerable work with it in the past thirty years, adapting it to the educational or training needs of specific groups and courses, refining and improving it as we became more familiar with the learning potential of this community-based orientation device. We regard the following elements as essential to the process:

1. Preparation. A thorough briefing is provided prior to The Drop-Off, giving the students a rationale for the process and a structural framework within which to work in the field. This is usually done through a chalkboard exercise and discussion in which the participants are asked to construct the development of a whole town from the earliest beginnings to the present. (See addendum for a detailed description of the chalkboard exercise.)

2. The Drop-Off Experience. The length may range from a half-day to two days. In extended training programs we have dropped off trainees for as long as two weeks, during which time they were supposed to study the town, find a place to live, and find a worthwhile job. The length depends on the nature of the program, the time available, and the results you are seeking. Participants are sent singly or in teams of three or four people.

3. Return and Initial Feedback. Immediate anecdotal feedback in both group discussion and individual discussion with staff is planned for the same day in all Drop-Off exercises to gain a quick overview of the experience and to get some of the stories out of

the way so that a more detailed analysis can be held in a subsequent session.

4. Detailed Analysis. The half-day drop-off groups are usually scheduled in such a way as to allow for a detailed analysis session the same afternoon or evening. For two-day groups, the detailed session is usually held the following day. In either case, this is done, at first, in a large discussion group of fifteen to twenty people, and then in smaller, more manageable groups for the last half of the session. The purpose of the session is to share perspectives and insights into the information-gathering process, the personal experience, and the elements of community.

5. Writing Reports. Each participant is asked to write a report covering two major areas: (1) facts, details, and information about the community studied and (2) the personal learning process and the skills developed.

For short-term orientation programs, when time is limited, we select a few small and medium-sized towns within a twenty- to thirty-mile radius, and devote one-half day to the drop-off. A one-hour briefing session is provided using the chalkboard exercise. Teams of students are dropped off in several towns or sometimes in a district, neighborhood, or a larger community. They are picked up three to four hours later, and the evaluation and feedback process begins. We do not require written papers in short programs.

In language-training situations overseas, we link The Drop-Off with language-acquisition assignments. For example, we use an orientation site each summer in Mexico, and language-class groups are dropped off in different towns three times per week for a half-day each, with specific language tasks to be performed in the course of the community investigation.

In longer programs, when time allows, a cross-cultural studies course may begin with a two-day drop-off in which students not only study the community, but must find a place to stay, and are expected to write detailed papers in addition to participating in a thorough feedback discussion with staff, faculty, and the entire class. The students are given a variety of options to pursue in writing their papers, but two elements are required: (a) information about the town and how it was derived and (b) a description of the personal learning and investigation process, with specific reference to the cross-cultural skills involved and how they were used.

One of the first reactions by participants is the discovery that the drop-off community, which resembles many other small towns a student has seen in this country, has its own special character. It has its own history, mood, sense of place, and social issues, if one explores below the surface. Students often learn more about the drop-off town in a few hours than they know about their own hometowns. It is not unusual for them to say that they intend to try the same process back home when they return.

Another benefit of the process is the experience of reaching out to strangers. Students often move in a tightly circumscribed world populated mainly by family, classmates, teachers, and friends. Some have limited contact with older people, the unemployed, children outside their own neighborhoods, and people of different economic classes or different social or cultural groups. This narrowness of experience is normal, but when it is transported overseas, many valuable learning opportunities are missed. The drop-off requires the participants to walk up to a variety of people, open conversations politely, show respect, seek information, modify their behavior, and make contact at a basic human level. The whole process of cross-cultural entry and reaching out to people comes into play. Students become conscious of their approaches to others and to life situations. They begin to be aware that there are some important skills involved and that they can personally develop and master these skills which then can be adapted and used overseas in the host community. Having practiced entry behavior and approaches in a "safe" exercise, the student tends to be less reluctant to approach unknown people and new situations in a host-country context.

Woven through the process is an effort to acquaint academically trained students with other modes of learning. While it is true that research and formal study skills are important, most overseas academic and exchange programs are not focused only on archival research and formal course work. Communication skills, problem-solving processes, and the whole panoply of field-learning techniques need to be employed if the student has any hope of experiencing the host culture in depth. The approaches which begin with The Drop-Off can be applied overseas to open up new avenues of inquiry, which serve to complement and enhance whatever formal course work is required by the specific program.

Addendum: Basic format for the chalkboard exercise used in briefing drop-off participants in Vermont:

You can help your group members see beyond the plane of surface immediacies with this fairly simple device. The theory is that if they are turning over a few good questions in their minds, if they want to find out something, they will have a more interesting experience and will be immeasurably more interesting to the local people they meet, precisely because they want to know something of value rather than just the location of the nearest beach or disco.

We start with a blank chalkboard, telling the group that we want them to help us fill in a "typical New England village" on the board. They mill around a bit and suggest a road or a house, but you have to push them further back in time. Gradually they get to hills, fields, trees, and perhaps a river, which is the way the town site was before European settlers arrived. Then you bring in the first settlers, the time period for New England being perhaps the mid-1700s, if not earlier. The group will want to set up some buildings, but the scattered farms come first, then the village green or common, where the cattle were kept in the early days. Then a few houses, plus a white frame church. By this time there will be a road or two, perhaps a bridge, and maybe a dam on the river for power as we move forward in time. A sawmill, possibly. A school. A store or two. Maybe a small bank. (You pull the answers out of them; don't give them away, although you may have to make some suggestions or give a few hints.) By now you are up into the 1800s, a large mill is built on the river, and new people come in to work there. The early settlers were probably Western European Protestants and have their own cemetery behind the white frame church. The new settlers are probably from Southern Europe, often Catholic, so they probably live in company housing near the mill and have their own church. And their own cemetery as time goes on. There are social outlets in such towns, usually unknown to modern students from suburbia: the Grange Hall and various other social clubs and associations (Red Men, Masons, Odd Fellows); then more stores and a town hall. There is probably a jail in the town hall by this time, and perhaps by now other industries and services have developed. The town would need a blacksmith, for example, and a farm equipment and grain supply store; and the townspeople may be converting their wood into furniture, bowls, and other salable items to bring in money. There is probably a bandstand on the village common, which is now used as a park and a centerpiece for the town, rather than a pasture. There would also be a war memorial commemorating those who served in the Civil War (and perhaps a World War I or World War II memorial of some kind). Times are changing rapidly on your chalkboard town plan as you move into the age of the automobile, which generates filling stations, garages, more roads and, ultimately, motels, restaurants, bars, roadhouses, etc. along the highway toward the next town. Another change is the fact that many of the people in this small town now commute to work in the larger town not far away. They also probably have built a large new school by this time, perhaps on some good flat land on the outskirts of town, with plenty of recreation area. And so on up to the present day, when the small industries may be changing with the changing times, dead drive-in theaters scar the scenery, and shopping malls and bowling palaces line the highway.

Having put the group through this process, which most of them enjoy, you are now free to reveal the framework underlying the questions you have been posing. You have a double acronym to work with: NAPI (nature, artifacts, people, information) and KEPRA (kinship, economy, politics, religion, and associations). Briefly stated, from this buildup and the outline, you can develop a great many questions about the town and its origins, who came there first, why they chose the place, what they did to survive, how they lived, how they amused themselves, how the place gradually grew and changed, etc. We start with a "typical New England village" because we in Vermont are surrounded by them and can easily take the groups to explore them with this workup as a guide. They are generally surprised at their own capacity to look at an unknown community with a fresh set of perspectives.

The next step is to transport the outline overseas. Either individually or jointly, students can try to see how a French or German town began (back to the river, hills, fields, forest, etc.), then the gradual increase in the population, and the development of the community into modern times. They will have to use the language to ask people questions. Host families might know some answers and might introduce them to others who know more, who in turn might open up the social history of the community, that vital past which brought the town to its current status and nourishes its values. As said before, most of the group have never looked at their own hometowns in this way, even the sociology and anthropology majors, and it is equally safe to assume they might never take this kind of look at their host communities or other towns overseas without the use of some device such as this one, which gives them a starting point.

Afterwards you can provide them with the NAPI and KEPRA scheme in the form of a grid arrangement which helps in the examining of the interrelatedness of the various elements of the exercise.[2]

	Kinship	Economy	Politics	Religion	Associations
Nature	_____	_____	_____	_____	_____
Artifacts	_____	_____	_____	_____	_____
People	_____	_____	_____	_____	_____
Information	_____	_____	_____	_____	_____

Any item in the vertical column can be examined in terms of its relation to any item (or each item) in the horizontal (e.g., Nature-Economy, etc.)

Notes:
  1. Desmond M. Connor, *Understanding Your Community* (Antigonish, Nova Scotia: D. M. Connor, 1964).
  2. The NAPI-KEPRA scheme appears in *Guidelines for Peace Corps Cross-Cultural Training,* Vol. 2 edited by Albert R. Wight and Mary Anne Hammons, (Estes Park, CO: Center for Research and Education, 1970), D 151-52.

14

Martian Anthropology Exercise

Donald Batchelder

This description is offered as an example of the kind of orientation activity which can be developed by any trainer anywhere. It can be staged in any setting, if one makes imaginative use of locally available resources, situations, and some imagination. The exercise places students into an active process which requires them to examine their ways of observing while trying out new methods. It was developed by Don Batchelder and Bill Harshbarger of The Experiment as a modified drop-off exercise which can be done in one and one-half to two hours and which is also fun to do. It places the participant in the position of being a stranger or an outsider looking at familiar things from a different point of view. The process worked as follows:

1. Group members are teamed in sets of two, three, or four people. The facilitator explains briefly that they are anthropologists from Mars, coming to this strange new culture (Earth) to examine aspects of the way of life and societal forms. The task is to harvest sufficient information for a high-level delegation planning a state visit to Earth in the near future. The Martian VIPs want to know

the important elements of life on Earth prior to starting the trip, and the group of anthropologists is an advance research team. After setting up the teams, the facilitator takes a few minutes to explain the scenario and to brief them with the following details of the exercise.

2. Each team or individual is given a handout suggesting the ways in which their observation and reporting should be carried out. The most effective reading for this is the well-known "Nacirema" article by Horace Miner.[1] Allow about fifteen minutes for the participants to read the article and to internalize the sense and style of it.

3. Assignments are then given to each of the teams. The following list will provide an idea of the kinds of assignments which work well. A few anecdotes are included with some of the items to give the reader an indication of the research findings to expect. The list is by no means exhaustive, but it may suggest excellent alternatives in the reader's locale.

   a. One team was recently sent to McDonald's for an hour to study *Family Life*. In addition to observing family roles, child rearing, and other phenomena, the team members introduced themselves as Martian anthropologists and interviewed several of the patrons and workers with good results.

   b. We usually send a team to a large bowling alley to study *Religion*. They immediately recognize the importance of the ten white icons at the end of each long aisle and report with considerable detail on the significance of the large spheres offered to the gods by the faithful, and the forms of physical and religious fervor displayed by the worshipers during the ceremony.

   c. Another group can be sent to a downtown bank to examine the *Education System*. They note that lessons are handled quickly by the educational institutions in this society; an exam form is swiftly filled out by the student, a brief report is handed to the teacher, who processes the exam or lesson through a machine and provides the student with paper vouchers in return. These vouchers, it has been noted, can later be exchanged for goods and services within the community, leading the Martians to the interpretation that there is a direct relationship between educational excellence and the society at large. Successful students are rewarded by the society in concrete terms.

d. A team is frequently sent to a supermarket to study *Agriculture and Food Gathering*. The researchers are often puzzled to find fresh fruits and vegetables growing in the absence of organic soil and seldom understand why the food seems to be covered by an invisible shield. They often deduce that the contents of food containers can be determined by the pictures on the outside of the containers, although this theory presents problems when the anthropologists pass along an aisle where baby foods or pet foods are displayed.

e. We generally send a team (depending on the ages in the group) to a workingmen's bar to study *Politics and Government*. They are quick to note the importance of the clear golden liquid which is used by the politicians in considering public affairs, and they are often impressed by the apparent fatigue of the rulers as they enter and their evident feeling of goodwill, well-being, and political accomplishment when they leave an hour later.

f. Teams have been sent to a local bookstore to study *Health and Medicine*.

g. We often send a team to the Laundromat to study *Science and Technology*.

h. Teams have been sent to a local ski area to study *Military Preparedness and Defense*.

i. Others have gone to the public library to see what they could learn about *Kinship Networks*.

j. A large discount store is often a good site for the study of *Recreation and Leisure-Time Activity*.

k. A paint and wallpaper store is an excellent place to examine *Art Forms, Fine Arts, and Cultural Expression*.

l. A music shop (instruments, compact discs, tapes, and stereo equipment) offers a fine vantage point for the study of *Economy and Business*.

m. A local gymnasium, recreation center, or health club is a good place to study *Social Organization*.

n. A hardware store or factory provides insight into the system of *Law and Justice*.

o. A busy bus station helps the Martians examine *Philosophical Thought*.

4. Pass out the assignments to each team on a slip of paper and dispatch them to complete their research tasks. They should take notepads and pens or pencils to record findings. Their task is to bring their research findings back and present them to a panel of Martian scholars.

5. Research period. One to one and one-half hours, depending on the time available.

6. Return to the orientation site. Give the teams enough time to assemble their data, over lunch or during the dinner hour, and then reconvene. Give each team about five minutes to report to the other groups in a large session. Members of other teams are free to comment and ask questions. All reports should be couched in terms parallel to the style used in Miner's "Nacirema" article (this needs to be stressed during the opening phase of the assignment).

7. After the five-minute reports, the research teams should be mixed. Working in new task teams, the group should try to prepare a concise briefing paper about each of the following important elements of life on Earth, based on what they have seen. One model is as follows:

• Hierarchical structure or system
• Communication
• Travel tips for the VIP Martian delegation: what gifts to bring, proper etiquette, etc.
• Time
• Ideals
• Attitudes
• Values
• Private and public behavior

Or, you can stop the process after the five-minute reports and have the participants discuss the following:

• the sensation of being a stranger and being stared at during one's study

- their inner feelings before and during the process and relating them to the upcoming overseas experience
- a comparison of our usual ways of seeing things (not noticing, being passive, being bored, taking for granted) with the Martian way (intense concentration on all features of assigned locale, attention to details) and the relevance of this to the field-learning situation overseas (observation skills, approaches to people and institutions, etc.)
- ways in which this process and variations on it can be used in a host-country situation. It should be stressed that this is not to satirize or make fun of anyone, but to transfer this kind of detailed observation skill (without the game element) into observation and information gathering in the host-country context

In addition to employing this device at orientation sites, we have used it in hotels at large conferences by sending teams to such places as the hotel beauty parlor, barber shop, bar, newsstand, gift shop, lobby, parking garage, kitchen, maid's supply center, and by riding an elevator for about half an hour. The topics to be examined in these locales can be decided at the time.

Results to be expected: The results are often mixed, but participants generally enjoy the exercise. The exercise itself moves along swiftly and, as in the case of most exercises, it is most important to have some structure to the discussion afterwards. There are some valuable lessons to be learned about the ways in which we observe and operate in a strange situation. Beyond this, the exercise has the effect of providing participants with a shared experience upon which to base a discussion. We use it at times to break participants out of the usual theoretical discussions and intellectualizing and to impress upon them the initiative and skills involved in trying something different, in getting outside of their usual modes and habits, and in standing back and gaining a different perspective.

Notes:
   1. Horace Miner, "Body Ritual among the Nacirema," *American Anthropologist* 58 (1956): 503-07.

15

Tisouro: **Creating Felt Needs**

by David Hopkins

Motivation is certainly one of the key elements of any training-teaming situation. We usually think of motivation as a desire to do (or understand) something. For the purposes of intercultural learning this needs to be defined more clearly. In the context of experiential learning it is not enough to think that we want to learn; we need to feel it. The result is what we call "felt needs," and the process of motivating learners is referred to as "creating felt needs." This means involving trainees/learners in a situation where they feel a need to learn or understand. Most effective simulations utilize the idea of creating felt needs, and the *Tisouro* (scissors, in Portuguese) exercise is a good example. This concept is better understood as an experience than as a theoretical discussion. The activity described below demonstrates how creating felt needs works using a simple and easy-to-conduct game.

The Scissors Game Objective

a. To make trainees aware that communication may include conflicting signals.
b. To focus attention on nonverbal behavior.
c. To explore the feeling of being included or excluded from a group.

Preparation:

Participants should sit on chairs in a circle. There must be enough space between chairs for people to turn and face each other during the game.

The only material needed is an ordinary pair of scissors. Group size should be under twenty.

Instructions:

This is a communication exercise. You will pass a pair of scissors around the circle in one of three positions: "closed," "crossed" (i.e., partially open), or "open" (i.e., wide open). (The facilitator demonstrates each position.)

Each time the scissors are passed, the passer must say how he or she is passing the scissors.

The receiver must then say how he or she is receiving the scissors: closed, crossed, or open.

The communication code is not exactly what it appears. You are encouraged to observe carefully as each person passes the scissors to discover the code.

Guidelines:

*   Do not discuss the code or process during the game.
*   Be sympathetic and friendly to others.
*   When you learn the code, help others to learn it but do so nonverbally, not by telling them.

The Code:

The scissors are passed and received according to how the legs of the sender and receiver are being held, not by the position of the scissors. The scissors are passed and received "open" if the sender's/receiver's legs are open; "crossed" if the legs are crossed; and "closed" if the legs are closed but not crossed.

Procedure:

a. The facilitator reads the instructions. When demonstrating the closed, crossed, and open positions of the scissors, the facilitator must subtly but clearly demonstrate the secret "code" by closing, crossing, or opening his or her legs. It is all right if some of the participants understand the code at this point.

b. The facilitator starts the process by passing the scissors to the first person to the right, stating how he or she is passing the scissors, (i.e., whether his or her legs are open, crossed, or closed). It is best at this point to have the scissors position correspond to that of the facilitator's legs.

c. The receiver takes the scissors and states how he/she is receiving them.

d. The facilitator should politely correct the receiver and each subsequent receiver and sender by stating how the scissors are passed according to the secret code. If the participant, whether by design or accident, uses the code correctly, the facilitator confirms it and congratulates the person.

Comments:

There will be some confusion initially, and participants will continue to be frustrated by the corrections of the facilitator. The facilitator must encourage those who understand the code to be helpful (nonverbally) to those who have not. Frustration will increase as more and more participants discover the code. The facilitator must be increasingly demonstrative in positioning his or her legs to assist the "out" group in understanding the communication process. It should be possible to get everyone to understand the code and join the "in" group before concluding the exercise. Be careful that those who do not "get it" are not embarrassed. The increasing peer pressure and frustration of those who do not understand increase the difficulty of discovering the code. This is a useful point for later discussion and relates clearly to the cross-cultural communication process.

The motivation for learning effectively exists within the exercise, but it must be explored. The felt needs created by the exercise make participants act or not act in certain ways and often create apparent understandings which may not be accurate. The discussion following the exercise helps participants sort out their reactions through sharing their experience with others.

Discussion:

The follow-up discussion is the key element in the exercise. The game should take fifteen to twenty minutes, depending on group size, but at least forty minutes should be allowed for processing it. This is particularly important when the frustration level is high. The facilitator can focus on the questions below as discussion starters, but should improvise as necessary.

Most of the processing questions are aimed at exploring the feelings of the participants as they played the game. These feelings create needs: the need to understand and be understood, the need to belong among those who understand the code (the "in" group), the need not to appear foolish, the need to go beyond the obvious to understand. Similarly, there may be a need to reject a situation which is uncomfortable, incomprehensible, or ambiguous. It is usually not necessary to be directive in pursuing the connection between the feelings created by the exercise and the need or motivation to do or not do something in response. Some participants are excited and challenged by the exercise, while others feel anger and alienation. Both reactions are typical of many cross-cultural interactions and should be explored. It is extremely important that the facilitator recognize all comments as being equally valid and valuable to the discussion and not try to lead the group to predetermined conclusions. The goal is for the participants to:

- Be conscious of the feelings that often accompany intercultural interactions
- Accept those feelings as real, legitimate, and permissible
- Realize that these feelings create needs to act or not act in certain ways
- Develop acceptable behaviors for dealing with these feelings

Sample Discussion Questions:
- How did you discover the code?
- How did you feel when you didn't understand the code?
- Did you feel a need to discover the code?

16

Examining Cultural Identity

Lise Sparrow

Over the years at The Experiment we have consistently found the exploration of cultural identity to be an essential ingredient in training intercultural professionals. Self-awareness is crucial to intercultural learning. Our predispositions, expectations, and reactions affect our perceptions. Our perceptions affect our judgments, how we solve problems and make decisions, and ultimately how we are perceived and trusted by others.

Because we are concerned with building quality relationships with our students and colleagues, we take time to hone our self-understanding and to acknowledge values and beliefs which may have become ingrained in our approach to relationships. From clarity about who we are and what we believe, we hope to better appreciate the perceptions of others and understand the mechanisms involved in moving beyond our private worldviews.

Each of the following exercises is intended to highlight one aspect of cultural identity. Using all of them allows participants to reevaluate themselves from a variety of vantage points, thereby highlighting the complexity of culture. Each one individually, how-ever, can provide its own window into aspects of the self which often go unexplored.

In all cases, thorough processing is essential. Participants need adequate time to consider what they have learned and to reflect on the activities themselves and on the cultural insights they provide. The exploration of cultural identity often brings forgotten memories or surprising insights to awareness, and they need to be fully acknowledged for learning to take place. The following descriptions include suggested ways of structuring and processing the activities. The precise form is far less important than that participants are given the support they need to draw out the learning which is inevitably present.

The activities are listed in an order which leads from general cultural values to more personal issues. This allows participants to get to know each other and build trust before entering into activities which demand a deeper level of sharing.

I. The Kluckhohn Questionnaire.

This is one version of a questionnaire that has been used in Peace Corps training since its inception. It derives its form from the paradigm developed by Florence R. Kluckhohn and Fred L. Strodtbeck in *Variations in Value Orientations* (New York: Row Peterson, 1961), in which they suggest that cultures can best be compared by examining five critical human dimensions: time, rela-tionship to nature, human nature, social relations, and form of activity.

Participants are asked to rate themselves in light of the beliefs they learned as children. Often, they repeat the exercise indicating what they believe now as adults and how their beliefs have changed since childhood. By asking them to assess the basic cultural attitudes they developed during childhood, subtle cultural influences may come to the surface which can be contrasted with the more conscious cultural values they now hold as adults. The exercise has also been used in processing cultural adjustment by asking participants to examine the host culture within this framework.

Cultural Value Orientations

Directions: Please mark the one statement in each category that best describes your culture's orientation. As a basis for your answer, try to remember what you were taught by your family, your religion, and your early schooling. Please do not answer with your *present* opinions, if they happen to differ from what you were taught. (These possible differences will be discussed later).

Time:
1. In my culture, people consider the past (tradition, history) the most important factor in making decisions.
2. In my culture, people consider the present (today and only today) as the most important factor in making decisions.
3. In my culture, people consider the future (what will happen) as the most important factor in making decisions.

Relationship to Nature:
1. In my culture, people consider themselves the victims of nature's forces.
2. In my culture, people consider themselves to be living in harmony with nature.
3. In my culture, people consider themselves to be in control of many natural forces.

Human Nature:
1. In my culture, it is thought that people, if not controlled, will probably act in evil ways.
2. In my culture, it is thought that people, if not controlled, will probably act in both evil and good ways.
3. In my culture, it is thought that people, if left to their own devices, will probably act in ways that are good.

Social Relations:
1. In my culture, people consider heritage and ancestry most important in their relationships to others.
2. In my culture, people consider their current extended family most important in their relationships to others.

3. In my culture, people consider the expression of individuality (in the context of a nuclear family) most important in their relationships to others.

Form of Activity:
1. In my culture, people think existing (being) is itself enough for life.
2. In my culture, people think that personal growth and development (being-in-becoming) is the most important goal in life.
3. In my culture, people think that practical action and accomplishment (doing) is the best goal.

Definition:
Cultural values have to do with what is judged good or bad, right or wrong, by a culture. They represent what is expected or hoped for, required or forbidden. Values are not behaviors themselves, but are the criteria, the bases, by which behavior is judged and sanctions applied.

Basic Attitude-Contrast Areas:
The underlying values of a culture may be viewed from the perspective of attitudes which predispose an individual to action. The following list of value contrasts was developed for Peace Corps training to examine the culture within the individual trainee by identifying attitudes with which he or she identifies. Circle the number of the choice which comes closest to where your belief lies on the spectrum between the contrasting values (e.g., in item no. 1, if you believe people are basically good, circle the 1; if you believe they are basically evil, circle 5; if your belief lies somewhere in between, circle 2, 3, or 4).

The Attitude toward:
1. People's basic nature: Basically good—Basically evil

    1   2   3   4   5

2. Life: All life highly valued—Individual less important than the group

   1   2   3   4   5

3. Death: Predetermined and inevitable—Accidental and haphazard

   1   2   3   4   5

4. Suffering and pain: To be avoided if possible—Inevitable and unavoidable

   1   2   3   4   5

5. Problem solving: Rational, logical—Instinctive, intuitive

   1   2   3   4   5

6. Status, titles, degrees: Attained for reasons other than merit—Earned by merit

   1   2   3   4   5

7. Animals: Having feelings similar to those of people—Having rudimentary feelings wholly unlike those of people

   1   2   3   4   5

8. Control of one's environment: Self-determined—Fatalistic

   1   2   3   4   5

9. Material objects: Highly valued—Not of great importance

   1   2   3   4   5

10. Science, technology, machines: Highly valued—Not of great importance

   1   2   3   4   5

11. Time: Present time valued—Concern and planning for the future

   1   2   3   4   5

12. Achievement: Goal-oriented—People-oriented
    1   2   3   4   5

13. Work: Brings tangible results—Valued for itself
    1   2   3   4   5

14. Manual work: For lower classes only—Good for everyone
    1   2   3   4   5

15. Value of experience: Learn by mistakes—Mistakes should be avoided at all costs
    1   2   3   4   5

16. Change: Possible with effort—Impossible to achieve
    1   2   3   4   5

17. Self vis-à-vis others: Privacy valued—Social interdependence valued
    1   2   3   4   5

18. Relationship with others: Independence valued—Group valued over individual
    1   2   3   4   5

19. Small group or family: These get strong and only loyalty—Other relationships valued as more important
    1   2   3   4   5

20. Community involvement: Little or none—Active
    1   2   3   4   5

21. Women: Inferior to men—Equal to men
    1   2   3   4   5

22. Relationships between the sexes: Platonic relationships possible—Sexual relationship always exists
    1   2   3   4   5

23. Relationships of the same sex: Close friendships—Close friendships uncommon

    1   2   3   4   5

24. Underdog: Sympathy—Scorn

    1   2   3   4   5

25. Authority: Resented, rebelled against—Valued, respected

    1   2   3   4   5

26. Meeting commitments: Casual, little concern—Great concern

    1   2   3   4   5

27. Bureaucracy and red tape: Acceptance—Can't tolerate

    1   2   3   4   5

28. Style of communication: Polite, vague, indirect—Frank, open,
direct

    1   2   3   4   5

29. Strangers: Complete distrust—Extreme hospitality

    1   2   3   4   5

30. Concern for status: No concern—Great concern

    1   2   3   4   5

31. Elders: Honor, respect, deference—Disrespect, distrust, disregard

    1   2   3   4   5

32. Classroom discipline: Very strict, reliance on punishment—
Very permissive, reliance on student responsibility

    1   2   3   4   5

We commonly process this activity by asking participants to
work in geographical, religious, or other groupings (e.g., Asians,
Europeans, U.S. Southerners, Californians, missionary/military,
New England Protestants, Jews, Catholics, etc.). They are asked to

compare their answers and to look for commonalities, which they then present to the large group. The small-group discussion often brings out meaningful anecdotes and highlights attitudes which may otherwise go unnoticed. When working with people raised in the U.S., this can provide a useful preview of American cultural traits.

II. Up-Down-Up

Though the format of this exercise may seem like that of a warm-up activity, it can have a powerful effect on individuals and the group. It provides a nice change of pace but needs to be used judiciously once students already know each other.

Students are asked to rise (and then sit back down) when they feel connected to any of the following aspects of cultural identity:

- Grew up in the suburbs, country, city.
- Only child, one sibling, two, three, etc.
- Nuclear family, extended family, commune, other?
- Protestant, Catholic, Jewish, Buddhist, Baha'i, etc.
- More than enough money, enough, not enough.
- Allowed to socialize with all friends, friendships limited, etc.
- Other aspects defined by teacher and/or raised by students. "Parent of one, two, etc. children" is a good one to add when adults are in the class.

As simple as it may sound, this activity gives participants the opportunity to become aware of aspects of their identity which, whether of little or great significance to them, stimulates reflection. The actual physical movement, for instance, causes participants to consider how they are perceived by others. The exercise also often spotlights, in a nonjudgmental manner, characteristics which are acceptable in one culture but considered wrong in another.

It is important to offer students an opportunity to suggest additional characteristics and categories to respond to. This gives the activity a spontaneous quality and helps make sure everyone feels included. The adding of other categories can illuminate dimensions of culture which may hold particular significance for individual students. It is also important to get the group to identify those aspects of culture which people might hesitate to name (divorce, homosexuality, etc.).

After the exercise, the group can be broken into pairs to discuss categories and characteristics that were of most significance. The large-group discussion can focus on more general issues, such as value contrasts, taboos, and labeling.

III. The Cultural Autobiography

This is another exercise which has been used over the years in a variety of ways but most often as described below. Participants are asked simply to jot down notes in journal fashion in response to a number of topics relating to their personal backgrounds and to discuss with a partner what they feel most interesting and significant about themselves. In other courses it has been used as a central assignment to be written and typed as part of a final synthesis demonstrating what has been learned. In every instance it provides a mechanism for systematically identifying factors which affected participants' acculturation and identity.

Cultural Autobiography

Think about yourself growing up, and make notes for yourself in your workbook on each of the subjects listed below. These notes are for you personally; you will be asked to talk from them but will not have to share them directly with anyone.

1. Family structure and relationships, role of parents, grandparents, and other family (including extended family) members.
2. Nationality(ies) of self, parents, grandparents.
3. Rituals of family life: daily living, special occasions.
4. Environment where you grew up: home, physical surroundings.
5. Friends: who, at what age, how long?
6. Individuals and/or institutions (church, college, etc.) which have had a strong influence on you.
7. Mobility: your own, your family's.
8. Education: where? how long? principal influences?
9. Other aspects of your life or influences upon it of importance to you.

IV. The Home Questionnaire

A related questionnaire is based on the ideas I encountered when Sharon Parks was teaching at the Harvard Divinity School. It requires that participants understand the somewhat abstract meta-phor which defines networks of significant personal relationships as a "tribal identity." The term is helpful in that it allows for the many cultural alternatives which exist today in the United States. Participants can define their "tribe" and cosmologies as they wish. This approach takes advantage of Native-American terminology to examine the interactions of participants' families and friends.

Recall an occasion in the not-so-distant past when you were "home." This can be with your family or with another group of people with whom you feel a sense of belonging.

Recall a specific occasion on which you were gathered together. If you cannot recall a specific occasion, imagine what you consider to be an accurate "generic" experience with your family/tribe. The assignment may also focus on a holiday or special occasion such as Thanksgiving, Christmas, Passover, or a wedding or funeral. Answer the following questions with this occasion in mind:

Questions: Please answer as completely as possible.

1. Who shared in the home experience on this occasion (not necessarily living under the same roof)?
2. What were the prevalent attitudes toward guests? Or who made up the "we" group, who were "they"? Describe the bounds of hospitality to others.
3. What of the past was important to the tribe?
4. What predictable rituals took place?
5. What other activities/entertainment took place? Who participated in what?
6. What roles did men take at the gathering? What roles did women take? How interchangeable were these roles? Describe the bounds of the roles.
7. Describe any traits (physical, behavioral, other) which might distinguish this tribe from others.
8. Who/what was the central force—the "god" perhaps—which held the tribe together and/or had meaning for all who gathered together?
9. Who/what were lesser "gods?"
10. Who was the "mud-god" (the reminder of the group's vulnerability)?

Note: The term "mud-god" is borrowed from the Hopi tradition to denote that against which the tribe unites. In the Hopi dance ceremony the dancers are costumed as the gods or *cochinas* and come together in unison as they throw mud at one particular figure which might represent the *black sheep* of the family or group, or a social or political belief or behavior which all join in rejecting.

Because this is a more personal activity, it is usually processed in pairs or triads. Participants are asked to share whatever strikes them as significant. As with any activity, it is important to emphasize that they need to reveal only what they wish or that to which they might like a response. In the large group it is appropriate to ask more general questions which seek out commonalities. For example, what types of persons or things were represented by the mud-gods? What kinds of roles were common? Did gender affect relationships? How helpful is the term "tribe," and how easy or difficult is it to identify one's own tribe? To what degree does the tribe reflect this or other cultures?

V. Spoon River Portrait

The name of this activity derives from the American classic, *The Spoon River Anthology* by Edgar Lee Masters. In it, Masters sketches (in poetry) the inhabitants of a fictional American small town, Spoon River. The book is frequently offered as reader's theater and this activity can be done in the same format. It allows students to appreciate the challenges of change and cultural adjustment and can provide a powerful group or personal experience. Here are the instructions.

Spoon River Portrait—A Life in Transition

The purpose of this assignment is for you to create a portrait, written as a first-person narrative or in free verse, approximately one, but no more than two, double-spaced pages in length. In this portrait, you describe an important transition in the life of one of your forebears.

The portrait describes aspects of your forebear's life as she or he experienced some kind of a transition or move. The account can be factual or it can be told as it may have been mythologized in your family. It should be written in the first person to capture this subject's voice. If at all possible, choose a person who, by virtue of an important decision, radically altered the course of her or his life, an immigrant, for example. Try to capture the "dream" of this person. Let us hear, through the narrative, about the values which served as a motivation during the transition and about what happened as a result.

Also let us hear how later circumstances may have shaped the dream and how at death the person may have evaluated the accomplishment of what he or she set out to do.

Optional Additional Instructions: You will be reading the portrait aloud in a sort of reader's theater tomorrow; please practice so you are prepared.

You will be asked to sit in a circle, read with expression, and reflect upon each reading before going on to the next. Once everyone has finished, you may ask questions of each other and then make comments on commonalities in content and on the impact of the exercise itself. Alternatively, this activity can be structured as a writing assignment to be handed in, read only by the teacher, and discussed in terms of what students learned from doing the activity.

In conclusion, these activities serve as catalysts for what can be a lifelong exploration of cultural identity. It needs to be kept in mind, however, that in each activity, whether completing the Kluckhohn questionnaire or writing the Spoon River Portrait, participants touch on both familiar and unfamiliar dimensions of themselves. Experiences of family, ethnic heritage, race, gender, sexual orientation, and trauma rise to the surface and can create the opportunity for sharing experiences and for individual learning. If handled with care, these insights can lay the groundwork for empathy, heightened sensitivity, and ultimately for improved intercultural relationships.

Part Three

ASSESSMENT

Introduction

Elizabeth Warner Christie

Experiential learning, as John Dewey has helped us realize, is marked by two important characteristics:

1. A rhythm of experience and reflection
2. A continuous interplay between the learner and what is being learned

What serves as a challenge to the assessment of experiential educational endeavors is the broad spectrum of learning resources that are drawn upon by the learner and the engagement of the whole person (or the whole "inner world" of the person—emotion, mind, and behavior) with those resources. Traditional methods for assessing cognitive knowledge (e.g., quizzes, examinations, papers, formal presentations) are not adequate for evaluating an individual learner's total experiential growth. We need techniques for assessing personal growth and maturity that address themselves in an integrated manner to the thoughts, feelings, and actions of the learner.

The Experiment encourages the development of approaches to experiential learning that are centered on the learner as a whole person. Learners therefore occupy the central role in the assessment process, as it is their goals and objectives and their progress toward those goals (as perceived by both themselves and others) that are at the core of the significant learning taking place. Acquisition of knowledge per se is only part of our focus. High priority is also placed on the development of personal skills and the commitment to apply both skills and knowledge in a responsible way vis-à-vis personal relationships and actions within a cultural context. Evaluation is seen not only as a definitive statement about what has been learned, but as a tool to help learners identify what still needs to be learned, what skills need to be gained if one's goals are to be realized. Our educational goal, therefore, is threefold:

1. that Experimenters will become self-sustaining learners capable and desirous of assuming responsibility for their own learning,
2. that Experimenters will gain an accurate insight into who they are as individuals and as members of a given culture, with a respectful appreciation for that culture and for the diverse cultures around the world, and
3. that each Experimenter will recognize the essential unity and interrelatedness of all peoples and will actively participate in helping to create a more peaceful world.

The articles that follow describe a number of approaches The Experiment has found helpful in assisting Experimenters to structure and understand their own learning within the cross-cultural context.

17

Assessing Experiential Learning Overseas

Bruce Wyatt

Periodic assessment of an individual's experiences is an integral part of The Experiment's overseas programs. To gain most fully from the cross-cultural context, participants are asked to set their goals, regularly reflect upon their experiences, analyze what and how they are learning, and record their impressions and thoughts. The focus of reflection is on three areas of learning:

Other	The new culture, its people and language, the other members of the group, American culture
Self	Values, emotions, one's identity as an American and as a world citizen
Nature of Learning	Methods of inquiry, communication, learning processes as experienced by the individual

While we consider these three areas of learning equally important, we find that growth of the participants in each area varies. Some of the factors causing this variation are (1) the students' prior experiences and knowledge, (2) their social and emotional maturity, and (3) their attitudes, motivations, and current interests. Built into each program are opportunities for the individual to grow in all three areas of learning at his or her particular level and pace.

Other, the first area of learning, is the one most easily assessed. Examples include understanding the relationship between the executive and legislative branches of the host government as well as understanding how electrical outlets and switches differ from our own. Students are encouraged to pursue learning about "other" through interacting directly with the culture and its people. For example, studies of agriculture are apt to take place through visiting or working on a farm and talking with the farmer and the neighbors as well as through studying development plans in a university library. Part of such learning comes from the comparative reflections on American agriculture, agricultural systems, or government. Temptations to make precipitous value judgments on the relative merits of the two cultures are tempered by the guidance and timely questions of the group leader.

The leader serves in many ways as a facilitator of learning, rather than a source of learning. She or he encourages participants to become more observant, to develop both curiosity and understanding of the host culture and of all they are experiencing. Group discussions provide testing grounds for impressions and ideas, helping group members learn from each other. Methods of stimulating inquiry might include identifying all the unfamiliar items in one's homestay setting and discovering their significance, or learning about current issues from newspapers, magazines, radio, and television and discussing these with homestay family members.

Students are asked to record their experiences in journals and in "critical incident" papers. They are often asked to design a project focusing on some aspect of the host community and share it with the group in one or more forms—sometimes oral or written, sometimes also visual (e.g., photographs, dance, drawings, mime) or gastronomic (the preparation of a cultural dish or meal for the group).

Perhaps the most dramatic learning, however, lies in the area of *self*. Participants are continually bombarded by new sensations and stimuli. They find themselves having confusing new feelings, experiencing new reactions, and developing different behaviors that seem necessary in the new culture. The old patterns, expectations, and cultural norms are no longer adequate, the old values no longer serve in exactly the same form. The leader works with the participants both individually and within the group to raise each one's general awareness of individual identity and of how all the new feelings and reactions can be understood and appreciated. During orientation at the beginning of the program, each student is asked to identify personal goals. The group develops group goals as well and, through various exercises and discussions, grows in its appreciation and understanding of the "cultural baggage" each member is bringing to this new experience—both the cultural values from their American context and the personal expectations and fears held by the individual. These perceptions and feelings are recorded in individual journals or "letters to self" that are read again at various points in the program, providing perspective on the changes and growth that are taking place.

The individual journal is perhaps the key tool for both the student and leader in assessing self-growth. Leaders often ask that the students share selected passages from their journals with them during the course of the program (honoring the individuals' right to keep private those entries they prefer not to share). In discussing self-growth, the leader helps the student to see the congruence between stated goals, declarations of growth, and actual behavior. It is not enough for the learner to say "I am becoming more patient" when just two days previously he or she stomped furiously around a bus station because the bus was two hours late (and the group leader had observed similar impatient behavior at the start of the program).

The experience is one that attempts to relate the learning about other and self to discovery of the *nature of learning*. Learning that is based on experiential, action-based opportunities taps ways of finding things out that are not called into play in the classroom setting. Language-training and cultural-orientation sessions, both prior to departure and throughout the program, help learners acquire culturally sensitive methods of inquiry and nonverbal techniques as well as verbal communication skills. The group leader helps students become more skillful in using different means of inquiry and in identifying the learning processes that work best for them.

Experiment programs are beginnings, not ends. We don't promise to deliver, at the end of a program, self-actualized experts on a foreign culture, fluent in its language and professionally skillful in working within its system. What we try to do is to move individuals toward becoming more responsible, sensitive, and knowledgeable world-minded adults.

18

Sample Formats from Experiment Programs

Evaluation
by Carol Jaenson

Like orientation, evaluation is an ongoing process. It is not something that happens once and then it's done. Rather, it is a continual assessment, a monitoring of growth, progress, and change that is taking place within the learner.

By its very nature, experiential learning is highly subjective when it comes to measuring what has been learned. It is virtually impossible to apply formal evaluative techniques (tests, quizzes, papers, etc.) to an academic program that is not structured in the traditional university classroom manner. What a student learns is often quite personal, divorced from what happens in the formal classes or seminars that may be a part of the program. Assuming that evaluation is important and necessary (and I strongly believe that it is), then new forms and new methods must be developed which are appropriate to this unique learning situation.

When I served as an academic director of The Experiment programs abroad, I was required to submit a formal letter grade with evaluative comments for each student upon completion of the program. More importantly, I was interested in how I could be most helpful to each student personally in reflecting upon and helping him or her synthesize what happened abroad in order for it to become a meaningful, lasting experience. Obviously, my own opinions of each individual were somewhat subjective. Therefore, I wanted students to consider evaluation from three different approaches: evaluation of themselves, other students' evaluations of them, and my own evaluation. I offered ongoing opportunities to students to give feedback to me as well.

I provided the following statement of expectations to each student, indicating what each would need to accomplish in order to complete the semester satisfactorily. At the same time, I expressed my openness to alternative ideas or suggestions.

Each participant will:

1. Give careful thought to and write down his or her personal goals and expectations for the homestay, seminar, and independent study periods.
2. Keep a journal for the duration of the program.
3. Demonstrate throughout the entire program the desire and interest to explore and integrate him- or herself into the local life and culture insofar as possible.
4. Write and contribute for discussion three critical incidents. (See "Using Critical Incidents"by Donald Batchelder (in this volume).)
5. Attend and actively participate in all seminar sessions and related group field experiences.
6. Be responsible for the material covered in the background readings.
7. Be responsible for one group briefing prior to a seminar session or direct a discussion related to a field experience or seminar topic.
8. Demonstrate, by a self-selected means, a comprehension of the information and ideas presented during the seminar and the ability to analyze them critically.
9. Demonstrate progress/growth in the use of cross-cultural skills.
10. Write an evaluation of his or her homestay experience and the seminar.

Responsibilities
Ronald Richardson and Jana Glenn-Carter

The following is an outline of an assessment approach used in a university-level study program in Caen, France. Within a broad framework emphasizing their *responsibilities*, students are informed at the beginning of the program about specific responsibilities within each aspect of the program.

Individual

1. Keep a journal, reflective and descriptive. Share selections with the group leader during three individual meetings.
2. Write and hand in "Personal Goals for the Semester" before departure.
3. Write and hand in three critical-incident papers, each about three pages.
4. Participate in one regular activity in Caen (such as cooking class, choir, theater or dance group, women's group, volunteer work in school or clinic).
5. Meet with the group leader for three individual sessions.

Group

1. Attend and participate in one group meeting each week.
2. Research human interest stories and historic information of one local area in the region of Caen. Go out and talk with people. Share the information at a group meeting.
3. Research one area on the group's travel itinerary; make arrangements for visits in the area; during the trip write a report to be handed in and presented orally to the group (about twenty minutes).
4. Talk with someone over fifty years of age about his or her personal experiences during World War II; describe the interview to the group.
5. Write and present, in French, an evaluation of a group "reunion" (about two pages) and present it to the entire group.

Seminar

1. Attend and participate in all classes, activities, and excursions.
2. Devise one creative project (it's up to you what you do with this; it could be visual, musical, nonverbal, or whatever you choose).
3. Write a one- to three-page critique of a creative project given by another group member and hand it in.

Independent Study Project

1. Take initiative necessary to implement your project; remain self-motivated and actively pursue the project goals; revise and refine your approaches as needed; try to relate your project to your experience of living in France.
2. Submit one written summary of your progress to the group leader before the group trip, describing where you are and your future plans.
3. Discuss the project regularly with the group leader as the semester progresses.

Evaluations

1. Write a two- to three-page critical evaluation of each of the following aspects of the Independent Study Program: (1) the orientation (due the first week in Caen); (2) the seminar (due the last day of the seminar); (3) the homestay (due the last week of the homestay); and (4) the program in general and the role of the group leader (due at the end of the program).
2. Remain active in process of self-evaluation and redefinition of goals throughout the semester. Discuss this process with the group leader during individual meetings.

General

1. Strive to take an active role in making yourself conscious of your development in self- and cultural awareness.
2. Orientation is an ongoing process throughout the program.
3. At the end of the program, a reorientation to the United States will attempt to deal with such questions as "What will I do if I return to the U.S. and people aren't very interested in my experience?"
4. Try to remember that a smile and a kind word can work wonders. Nurture patience.

What Is Being Learned on an Experiment Program?

From materials provided to group leaders

Many educational systems say: "Learn this, study these materials, master this unit of learning." The Experiment is saying: "See for yourself, experience it, live it totally, learn by sharing the lives of others."

An essential step in learning from experience is taking time to reflect on those experiences and understand what they mean. This is what makes the difference between simply "doing The Experiment" or "living through it" and actually learning from it, having it make a positive contribution to one's life. We ask both leaders and group members to assume responsibility for taking this step and to reflect on what they are learning:

- about the world outside (the host culture, each other, the U.S.) from their new perspective
- about themselves, their inner worlds (values, emotions, identity)
- about new ways of learning (inquiry, participation, trying new things)

As leaders and group members develop their own ways of reflecting on their experiences, we ask that they bear in mind certain principles we have found to be essential to fruitful assessment:

1. Assessment of learning is a continuous process; evaluative questions need to be introduced at the start of the program and raised throughout.
2. The prime evaluator is the learner, who has the right and the responsibility to define and modify goals throughout the program and the prime responsibility for assessing his or her experiences.
3. Each learner is taken to be a unique individual. Therefore any evaluation must be based on that individual's performance and learning, not on the attainment of an absolute goal.
4. The purpose of evaluation or assessment is to offer supportive feedback so that the learner has more accurate perceptions of his or her strengths and of those personal areas that need to be strengthened.

5. Evaluation is open and honest; there are no secret files or opinions; there is constructive exchange between leader and Experimenters so that learning and growth may take place.

MEMO TO EXPERIMENTERS

How Can You Help Your Learning Take Place?

The Experiment encourages leaders and group members to be creative in designing a process of learning that meets their individual purposes. At the same time, we ask you to meet one of our needs as an organization: to assess how well educational goals of the program are being realized and to understand how the learning experiences of present Experimenters can help future participants to learn.

The list of questions below is designed to stimulate your thinking; the Evaluation Card enables you to share your written assessments with us at the end of the program. In addition to this written feedback, we invite you to develop other ways to further your learning. The following techniques have been found to be valuable: journal writing (individually and as a group), group discussions to share perceptions and give feedback to each other, individual discussions between leader and program participants focusing on such things as growth and the realization of personal goals, taping group discussions for later listening, and having the group complete an Evaluation Card on how effectively the leader has helped group members learn from their experiences.

Questions to Think About

What am I learning?
   What do I know about the host country that I didn't know last month? Last week?
   How have my impressions of the host country changed in the last week? Why?
   How do I feel about this place? These people? Why?
   What am I learning about my own country by being here?
   What am I learning about myself and the U.S. from my group?
   What am I trying to learn?
   What could I learn if I wanted to? How? Who could help me?

How am I fitting in?
Do I like the host culture? Yes? No? Not sure? Why?
Am I making new friends and acquaintances? Who are they?
Am I reaching out to others? Trying new things?
Am I fully involved/partially involved/hanging back? Why?
Is my host family enjoying my presence? Why do I think so?
Which of my habits and behaviors are suitable or acceptable to them? Why?
Which habits and behaviors should I change? How can I find out?
What can I give or do to make my being here a better experience for my hosts?
Am I participating in things my hosts enjoy?
What new ideas or ways of looking at things have I seen/heard/observed/tried?

How am I communicating?
Am I communicating successfully in the language?
Am I communicating successfully in gestures, attitudes, behaviors, facial expressions?
Am I listening carefully? Tuning out?
Am I demonstrating by my behavior that I like my hosts, appreciate their hospitality, am happy to be here, like their country? How? Smiles? Words? Actions?
How could I learn to communicate more effectively? Who could help me?
What can I learn from the experiences of the other group members?

How am I learning?
What do I see, hear, read, experience, discuss, ask, remember?
What has happened?
How have I reflected on it?
What inquiries have I made?
What would I like to find out? How? Who could help me?

How does this experience and how do these people relate to me and my life?
What are the five most important things I have seen, learned, experienced?
What have I learned about myself as a result of this experience?
How do I feel about what I saw, learned, experienced, and why?

How do I feel about the relationships I have established? About those I return to?

How do the values I have discovered here relate to my previous values?

What new values do I take home with me?

In adapting to and learning from this culture and the group, have I developed the potential of living more fully in my own culture?

What of my experience can I share with friends and family at home? How?

What new perspectives do I have on my own family? My community? My country?

What new ideas do I have about the nature of the contemporary world? The nature of human beings?

Evaluation Cards

The group leader is asked to fill out a card for each student.

Last Name	First Name	Town	Country	Year
Birth Date	Program	Semester	Leader	

Please describe your perception of the Experimenter's experience during the program, what he or she has learned from the experience. In doing so, please refer to the sheet "What Is Being Learned on an Experiment Program?" and consider some of the questions raised therein. Please also comment specifically on the Experimenter's adjustment to the host family and culture, use of foreign language, and inner growth and maturity.

To the Experimenter: Please refer to the questions raised for your consideration in "What Is Being Learned on an Experiment Program?" and share your perceptions of what you have learned during this program, how you have learned it, how you have grown. (Note: We will be asking for your evaluation of the program after you return home.)

Your Objectives, Guidelines, and Assessment (Y.O.G.A.)

Alvino E. Fantini

Background and Purpose

In providing foreign-language instruction, we initiate a process of learning which normally continues abroad. Our concern is with the immediately practical goal of helping the student to communicate in a foreign culture.

This instrument is provided as a means of effectively assessing one's progress at any point in time and may be used in combination with more traditional types of language testing. It has a three-fold purpose:

1. As a statement of objectives which expresses what we believe are the minimal attainable goals for survival language needs;
2. As a guideline for observation, directing both the learner's and the teacher's attention to the learning process in an effort to determine what progress is being made in the direction of the stated objectives; and finally,
3. As an assessment tool for evaluating whether the individual participant has attained those objectives.

The Components

The instrument addresses three aspects of communicative competence.

Note: The stages listed at the end of each of the three parts refer to the stages in developing intercultural communicative competence discussed in the author's article appearing in this volume, "Focus on Process: An Examination of the Learning and Teaching of Intercultural Communicative Competence."

PART I: Language Proficiency

Specific linguistic features of grammar, vocabulary, and pronunciation are evaluated to determine how well the student masters actual language (aside from his or her ability to communicate through other means) (Stages one, two, three).

PART II: Behavioral Performance

In this section, the individual's ability to perform (or to communicate in a more general sense) is distinguished from the ability to speak the language accurately, since some people are capable of communicating fairly well with only minimal language by resorting to nonlinguistic means such as gestures, body language, etc. The emphasis is on determining what one can do with what one has learned (Stages four, five).

PART III: Attitude toward the Host Language and Culture

The learner's attitude toward the target language often reflects more general attitudes toward the host culture. These attitudes directly affect one's proficiency in learning the foreign language. This section is normally used only by the learner (and academic leader), since teachers do not normally have an opportunity to observe their students abroad (Stages six, seven).

Combined, these three aspects help the development of intercultural communicative competence, an ability which is indispensable in helping the learner participate effectively in the host culture on its own terms.

When Is the Form Used?

Since the instrument expresses instructional goals, it is important for teachers, leaders, and students to become familiar with its contents from the onset of the language course. As it is also a guideline, it should be referred to continually throughout the language course and the experience abroad as well as after the program, when the student, we hope, will maintain an interest in and study of the target language and culture.

As an assessment tool, however, the Y.O.G.A. is to be filled out by students and reviewed with teachers at the end of the intensive language course. At this stage, only parts I and II apply. Students with previous knowledge of the language should also be evaluated within the first few days of the program to provide a basis for measuring progress. Before the end of the program abroad, the student and leader will assess the student's competence one last time.

Given the nature of the instrument, it is not necessary to evaluate the students in a specially controlled test situation. Rather, the student reflects on his or her ability at a given time, fills out the evaluation, and teacher and student review it together. In some cases, however, in order to complete part II, the leader or teacher may wish to spend fifteen or twenty minutes probing the learner's control of specific linguistic features.

Instructions for Using the Y.O.G.A. Form

Because of its threefold purpose, this instrument should stimulate continuing discussions and feedback among teachers, leaders, and students.

Each student has a Y.O.G.A. form which is filled out at the end of the language course and again at the end of the overseas experience. Students with previous knowledge of the language also complete forms at the beginning of the language course. In all cases the procedure is the following: the student assesses him- or herself by completing this form. Then the teacher and/or leader reads over the self-evaluation and discusses it with the student, incorporating any changes which they have agreed upon in accordance with the system described on the following page.

Code: Use a check mark at the beginning of the language program.

    0   1   2   3   4   5

Use an X at the end of the language course.

    0   1   2   3   4   5

Use a circle at the end of the stay abroad.

    0   1   2   3   4   5

If the teacher/leader disagrees with the assessment of an item made by the student, he or she may give an opinion after discussion with the student by crossing out the student's assessment, adding his or her own, and initialing the change in the margin.

PART I: Language Proficiency

This section focuses on the linguistic content of communication, i.e., how accurately you control the language. The items below are concerned with comprehension, fluency, pronunciation, vocabulary, and basic sentence patterns. Use the following scale, keeping in mind the relevant criteria.

Another way to rate yourself accurately is to compare your knowledge in your native language with knowledge of the target language.

0. Oral language not attempted.
1. Oral language reflects knowledge of theoretical use, but real and practical knowledge is still lacking.
2. Fair approximation of native speech; intelligible but with difficulty.
3. Good approximation of native speech; intelligible, but with some hesitation at times.
4. Excellent approximation of native speech; occasional slight errors.
5. Extremely close approximation of native speech characteristics; consistently excellent in all respects.

Remember that as you make progress, the time it takes to go from one number to the next becomes longer. Rate yourself on each of the following items:

1. How well do you understand the host language spoken to you at slightly slower than normal speed?

   0   1   2   3   4   5

2. How intelligible is your pronunciation?

   0   1   2   3   4   5

3. How fluent is your use of the host language (i.e., how much hesitation or stumbling is there)?

   0   1   2   3   4   5

4. How adequate is your vocabulary in performing those tasks appropriate to your level (see part III)?

   0   1   2   3   4   5

Rate knowledge of vocabulary in the following areas:

5. Days, months, seasons

   0   1   2   3   4   5

6. Family relationships (e.g., mother, father, etc.)

   0   1   2   3   4   5

7. Parts of body

   0   1   2   3   4   5

8. Parts of house

   0   1   2   3   4   5

9. Clothing

   0   1   2   3   4   5

10. Social expressions (e.g., hello, good-bye, thank you, etc.)

    0   1   2   3   4   5

11. Interrogatives (e.g., who, what, etc.)

    0   1   2   3   4   5

12. Expressions of time/place (e.g., yesterday, next week, there, upstairs, etc.)

   0   1   2   3   4   5

13. Cardinal numbers (e.g., one, two, etc.)

   0   1   2   3   4   5

14. Ordinal numbers (e.g., first, second, etc.)

   0   1   2   3   4   5

15. Geographic directions (e.g., north, south, etc.)

   0   1   2   3   4   5

How well are the following sentence types formed:

16. Simple affirmative statements

   0   1   2   3   4   5

17. Simple negative statements

   0   1   2   3   4   5

18. Simple questions

   0   1   2   3   4   5

19. How correct is the word order in the sentences you form?

   0   1   2   3   4   5

Now judge how well you use and exercise control over the following features of the host language—if applicable to it:

(Beginners rate themselves at the end of formal instruction on items 20 through 25 only. Low-intermediate students rate themselves before formal instruction begins on items 20 through 25):

20. Personal pronouns (e.g., I, you, she, etc.)

   0   1   2   3   4   5

21. Verbs—a form of the present tense

| 0 | 1 | 2 | 3 | 4 | 5 |

22. Definite articles (e.g., "the" in English; *la, il* in Italian, etc.)

| 0 | 1 | 2 | 3 | 4 | 5 |

23. Indefinite articles (e.g., "a, an" in English; *un, una* in Spanish, etc.)

| 0 | 1 | 2 | 3 | 4 | 5 |

24. Gender and number of nouns

| 0 | 1 | 2 | 3 | 4 | 5 |

25. Possessives (e.g., my, your, etc.)

| 0 | 1 | 2 | 3 | 4 | 5 |

(Beginners rate themselves at the end of the program abroad on all previous items, plus items 26 through 31. Low-intermediate students rate themselves at the end of formal instruction on all previous items, plus items 26 through 31.)

26. Noun case endings (as in German, Polish, etc.)

| 0 | 1 | 2 | 3 | 4 | 5 |

27. Verbs—a form of the past tense

| 0 | 1 | 2 | 3 | 4 | 5 |

28. Prepositions (e.g., with, for, to, etc.)

| 0 | 1 | 2 | 3 | 4 | 5 |

29. Verbs—a form of the future tense

| 0 | 1 | 2 | 3 | 4 | 5 |

30. Expressions of time

| 0 | 1 | 2 | 3 | 4 | 5 |

31. Noun-verb agreement

| 0 | 1 | 2 | 3 | 4 | 5 |

(Intermediate students rate themselves at the end of the program on all previous items, plus items 32 through 40. All students are encouraged to look at and rate themselves on any items they have worked with.)

32. Contractions (e.g., I don't, I'm)

   0   1   2   3   4   5

33. Reflexive verbs (e.g., *acostarse* in Spanish)

   0   1   2   3   4   5

34. Direct object pronouns (e.g., I read the book, I love her)

   0   1   2   3   4   5

35. Verbs—a form of the conditional (I would go)

   0   1   2   3   4   5

36. Verbs—progressive tenses (I am eating)

   0   1   2   3   4   5

37. Adjectives—comparative, superlative forms (big, bigger, biggest)

   0   1   2   3   4   5

38. Indirect object pronouns (equivalent of "to him, to us," etc.)

   0   1   2   3   4   5

39. Verbs—a form of the imperfect (*she was reading when I came*)

   0   1   2   3   4   5

40. Relative pronouns

   0   1   2   3   4   5

41. Verbs—a form of the subjunctive

   0   1   2   3   4   5

42. Indirect speech (e.g., Nancy said she was going)

   0   1   2   3   4   5

43. Passive voice

0	1	2	3	4	5

PART II: Behavioral Performance

This part deals with your ability to perform any of the tasks cited; whether you do so through oral language or other means is not the point but, merely, can you communicate? Using the scale, first determine whether the student has had experience with the situation, and then rate relative ability to communicate from (5)—complete ability (i.e., on a par with a native speaker) down to (0)—no ability.

Note: this section is divided into three parts. Beginning students in the language should have been exposed to and be able to deal with all of the tasks from 1 to 6 at the end of a 90-hour language course and all of the tasks through 10 by the end of a summer program abroad.

Intermediate students should be able to do any of the tasks from 1 to 16 at the end of a 90-hour course and from 17 to 26 by the end of a program abroad.

Advanced-intermediate students should be able to perform all of the tasks included in the list.

1. How well can you give or ask for directions?

0	1	2	3	4	5

2. Can you ask and tell the time of day, day of week, date?

0	1	2	3	4	5

3. Can you order a simple meal alone?

0	1	2	3	4	5

4. Can you make purchases (food, clothing, tickets) on your own?

0	1	2	3	4	5

5. How well can you respond to biographical questions (about nationality, marital status, occupation, date of birth, etc.)?

0	1	2	3	4	5

6. Can you get around alone by bus, train, taxi, etc.?

| 0 | 1 | 2 | 3 | 4 | 5 |

7. How well can you handle currency?

| 0 | 1 | 2 | 3 | 4 | 5 |

8. Can you ask and obtain biographical information from others?

| 0 | 1 | 2 | 3 | 4 | 5 |

9. How well can you handle yourself in social situations (with appropriate greetings, social introductions, and leave-taking expressions)?

| 0 | 1 | 2 | 3 | 4 | 5 |

10. How well can you assist someone else who does not know the language in coping with the above situations or problems?

| 0 | 1 | 2 | 3 | 4 | 5 |

11. How well can you describe, in some detail, your present or most recent job or activity?

| 0 | 1 | 2 | 3 | 4 | 5 |

12. How well can you provide detailed information about your family, home, or hometown?

| 0 | 1 | 2 | 3 | 4 | 5 |

13. How well can you give a brief autobiography and tell of your immediate plans and hopes?

| 0 | 1 | 2 | 3 | 4 | 5 |

14. How well can you speak of your experiences in your host family, host community, or host country?

| 0 | 1 | 2 | 3 | 4 | 5 |

15. How well can you use the systems of measurement in your language of study (distance, time, weight) to express your ideas?

| 0 | 1 | 2 | 3 | 4 | 5 |

16. How well can you describe the purpose or function of The Experiment/World Learning program and/or organization?

   0   1   2   3   4   5

17. How well can you describe the geography of the United States or some other geographic location?

   0   1   2   3   4   5

18. How well can you describe the basic structure of the U.S. government or educational system?

   0   1   2   3   4   5

19. How well do you understand what native speakers tell you, and how well do they understand you?

   0   1   2   3   4   5

20. How well can you take or give simple messages over the phone?

   0   1   2   3   4   5

21 How well can you follow and contribute to a conversation among native speakers?

   0   1   2   3   4   5

22. How well can you handle yourself with a group of educated native speakers?

   0   1   2   3   4   5

23. How well do you handle yourself socially with your hosts, without offending or irritating them linguistically?

   0   1   2   3   4   5

24. How well can you take notes and summarize an informal discussion?

   0   1   2   3   4   5

25. Can you serve as an informal interpreter on any of the above topics?

   0   1   2   3   4   5

PART III: Attitude toward the Host Language and Culture

This part assesses your attitudes toward the host language and culture. Hence, it is a relative assessment on a scale ranging from "not at all" to "some" to "a lot." These ratings in themselves mean little; yet in comparing your feelings at the beginning to those at the end of a sojourn abroad, you may better monitor your attitudes and their effects on your learning and on improving your communicative skills.

Unlike other parts of this form, there are no specific goals to be reached. "Some" or "a lot" may be realistic reflections of the successful sojourner's experience, but so may "not at all." However, answering the questions below may help you to reflect upon your experience and to gain more from it.

Obviously this section is to be marked only during and after a sojourn abroad.

	not at all	some	a lot
1. How well did you adjust to the host culture?			
2. To what extent was your attitude toward host nationals favorable?			
3. How much did you attempt to be with host nationals?			
4. How well did you get along with your host family (if applicable)?			
5. How much did you attempt to identify with the host culture?			
6. How much did you try to use the host language?			

Reporting of Language Assessment

Once the form has served as a checklist (for students, teacher, and leader) and as a focal point for evaluation and assessment of language progress, the student and leader (or teacher) make a final and comprehensive assessment of language development.

The leader (or teacher) is responsible for writing a narrative comment summarizing the student's progress and describing his or her communicative competence to determine whether credit is to be granted for language. The form below should be filled out and sent to the Department of Language-Culture Studies.

— —

Assessment of Communicative Competence

To: DEPARTMENT OF LANGUAGE-CULTURE STUDIES
      SCHOOL FOR INTERNATIONAL TRAINING
      BRATTLEBORO, VT 05302

Date _____

Student's Name _____
                     (first)   (last)

Language_____

Teacher_____Leader_____

Host Community and Country _____

Level (check one): (   ) Beginning
                    (   ) Intermediate
                    (   ) Advanced

Please describe in sufficient detail the student's growth and progress in communicative competence as reflected in the Y.O.G.A. forms, i.e., (1) Language proficiency; (2) Behavioral performance; and (3) Attitude toward the host language and culture.

   MERITS LANGUAGE CREDIT?   Yes ___   No ___

About the Authors

In the fifteen years since *Beyond Experience* was first published, the lives of the authors have changed along with the times. Many are no longer associated professionally with World Learning, Inc. the new name for The Experiment, although they stay in touch. A few have even dropped out of sight, and we reprint their work in hopes they will be pleased when we next see them.

Donald Batchelder, who was joint editor of the original edition, has recently headed the country program in Mozambique for Save the Children. Another former staff member, **Janet Gaston**, is now manager of training for the city of Richmond, just south of Vancouver, British Columbia. After a number of years at Mount Holyoke College, **Bruce Wyatt** has recently become vice president for external affairs at Beloit College. **William Dant** continues his involvement in international programs at Youth for Understanding in Washington, D.C. **Elizabeth Warner Christie**, joint editor of the first edition, has been active in community-service work in Brattleboro, Vermont. After a number of years in The Experiment's Projects in International

Training and Development, **Carol Jaenson** is now working on AIDS-related projects in Uganda with Family Health International. **Anne Janeway** remains in touch with World Learning on a project basis, most recently coteaching the cross-cultural course in the Master of Arts in Teaching Program at the School for International Training (SIT). Retired from the The Experiment in the U.S., **John Wallace** spent several years as secretary-general of the Federation of National Representations of The Experiment in International Living and is active on the boards of a number of educational and cultural organizations in Vermont and the Virgin Islands. **David Hopkins**, with an Experiment background both as student and staff, is currently teaching at Chubu University in Japan. The editor of this new edition, **Theodore Gochenour**, maintains a consulting relationship as senior advisor to World Learning.

Two of the original authors are still with World Learning on a regular basis. **Alvino Fantini** teaches Bilingual-Multicultural Education in the Master of Arts in Teaching Program at SIT and served as president of the International Society for Intercultural Education, Training and Research in 1991-1992. For many years, **Claude Pepin** has managed the Southeast Asian refugee training program and serves as vice president for Organizational Development and Planning. On the staff of the School for International Training are **Karen Blanchard**, faculty member of the Program in Intercultural Management, and **Lise Sparrow**, who teaches in the Master of Arts in Teaching Program.

We were unable to locate **Gordon Murray**, formerly director of The Experiment's Academic Studies Abroad Program in Nepal.

Our thanks to all of those whose contributions have made a revised edition of *Beyond Experience* possible.